IN THE DEVIL'S DOMINIONS

A UNION SOLDIER'S ADVENTURES IN "BUSHWHACKER COUNTRY"

Charles W. Porter

To Herbert H. Davis

And

To The Memory of

Gordon C. Davis

IN THE DEVIL'S DOMINIONS

A UNION SOLDIER'S ADVENTURES IN "BUSHWHACKER COUNTRY"

The Journal of Charles W. Porter
Lieutenant, Afterwards Captain
Co. F, 3rd Wisconsin Cavalry
Stationed in Southwest Missouri
1862-1865

Original Journal Located by
Herb and Gordon C. Davis
at the
State Historical Society of Wisconsin
Madison, Wisconsin

Transcribed by Volunteer Staff
Fort Scott National Historic Site
Fort Scott, Kansas
Arnold Schofield, Historian

Edited and Annotated by
PATRICK BROPHY

BUSHWHACKER MUSEUM
VERNON COUNTY HISTORICAL SOCIETY
INC NOT FOR PROFIT
NEVADA, MISSOURI

Cover Painting
In The Devil's Dominions
By Ed Koski

ISBN 1-893046-10-9

Library of Congress Catalog Card Number
98-74036

Published By
BUSHWHACKER MUSEUM
« Vernon County Historical Society »
INC. NOT FOR PROFIT
231 North Main Street
Nevada, Missouri 64772

TABLE OF CONTENTS

Porter's Journal

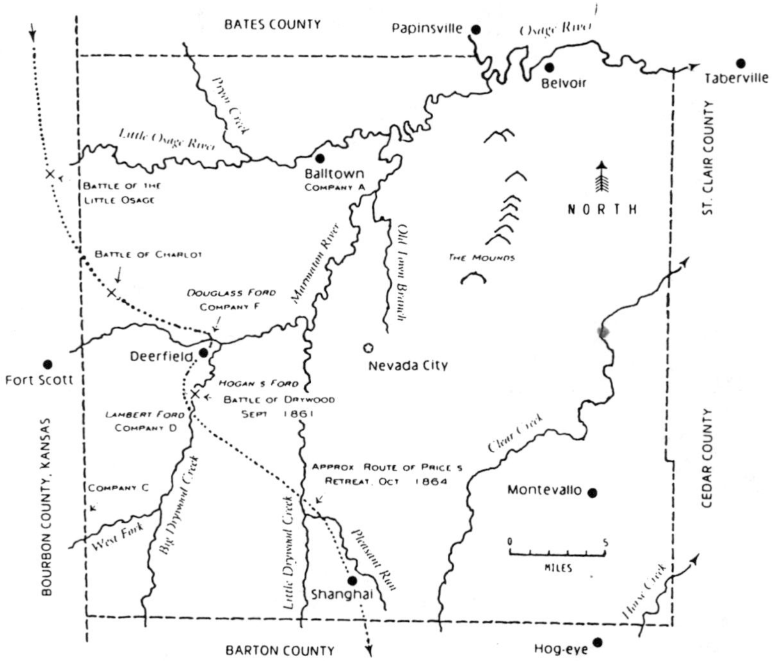

VERNON COUNTY, MO., IN THE 1860s

LOCATION MAP
SETTING OF
PORTER'S JOURNAL

❦ FOREWORD ❦

By The Editor

Brothers Herb and the late Gordon C. Davis were rummaging through the archives of the State Historical Society of Wisconsin in Madison, hot on the cold trail of their long-lost great-uncle Hiram C. Davis, when they stumbled on the manuscript journal of Lieutenant (afterwards Captain) Charles W. Porter, of Company F, 3rd Wisconsin Cavalry Regiment, rather cumbrously entitled *A Journal of Events in the Life of Charles W. Porter While in the Service of the United States During the Rebellion.*

The Davises' grandfather, Simeon Bennett Davis, had served with the 3rd Wisconsin in Missouri and actually met and married their grandmother, Sarah Emaline Garrison, there. Hiram C., Simeon's younger brother, had disappeared from home during the war, never to be heard from again. It was always presumed that he had run off to the war, enlisted under an assumed name, and then died and was buried under that name.

Porter's journal provided stunning confirmation. On November 9, 1863, Porter wrote, "One of my Company by name of Johnson is very low with Typhoid fever." Next day he added, "This morning at 3 O'clock 15 minutes, John H. Johnson *proper name Davis* [emphasis added] died of Typhoid fever. . . . The name of Johnson he assumed when he enlisted as he ran away from home, and took this precaution that his parents might not find him." On the 11th, following the burial in "the little Cemetery near Balltown," the diarist further noted, "He had one brother in our company to mourn his loss."

The modern Davis brothers visited Balltown Cemetery, and there, in the Civil War plot, found the gravestone of John W. Johnson. With the aid of Arnold Schofield, historian at the Fort Scott (Kansas) National Historic Site, they obtained a new government marker bearing the correct name. It was unveiled—alongside the old—on September 19, 1992, in a colorful full-dress reenactment of a Civil War-era military funeral.

That was only the beginning of interest in the Porter journal. Eagerly Schofield obtained a copy of the longhand original from the Wisconsin archives, and volunteer personnel at the National Historic Site spent a matter of years making a painstaking computer transcription. A 400-page printout was presented to the Bushwhacker Museum, located in the Missouri county just nextdoor, where the diarist spent most of the war—and incidentally, like the Davises' grandfather, found a wife.

Charles W. Porter was 30 years old, a resident of Baraboo, Wisconsin, when the Civil War broke out in April, 1861. He promptly enlisted, and as promptly began keeping a journal, which he continued throughout his period of service. Not a day went by when he failed to find time for a detailed entry.

The only personal fact about him disclosed by the journal, aside from his age, is his weight: 170 pounds. The journal does tell us he had a brother, Walworth D. Porter, serving as a sergeant in the same unit. The diarist took his new wife back to Wisconsin at the end of the war, and there—alas—drops from the record.

Porter first enlisted in the 1st Wisconsin Infantry, and served his three-months' enlistment term in the Eastern theater, in Maryland and Virginia. In August, 1861, he returned to Wisconsin, and on November 4 enlisted again, this time for a three-year term, in a company being raised by Captain David S. Vittum for the 3rd Wisconsin Cavalry. He was made orderly sergeant, and later commissioned second lieutenant and ultimately captain.

The regiment spent the entire war in the West, based at Fort Scott, a frontier military post abandoned in 1854 but reactivated in 1861 in the midst of the town that had sprung up on the site—"one of the growing towns of the territory," even in 1860, according to the Westport (Mo.) *Weekly Border Star.* And like other Kansas towns, it "boomed with the outbreak of the war." "In the summer of 1863 it had a population of between one and two thousand permanent residents and as many more transients," according to Albert Castel *(A Frontier State at War).* "It was a 'fast town,'" noted for "horse races, fights and drunken sprees," and boasting "numerous 'best saloons,' a dozen or so billiard parlors and bowling alleys, and a theater in a barn. . . ."

The regiment traveled by rail to Chicago and St. Louis, suffering a train wreck enroute and long delays for training in camps at either end. Mustered into U.S. service on January 4, 1862, they went on by steamboat to Fort Leavenworth, in northeast Kansas, and at last struck out overland south for Fort Scott.

Some companies of the regiment were stationed farther south, keeping Federal communications open with Fort Smith in Arkansas and Fort Gibson in the Indian Territory. The majority worked in and around Fort Scott itself, their primary duty being to "keep back" the Confederate Bushwhackers, or guerrillas, rife in nearby western Missouri. Their duties took them as far south as Fort Smith in Arkansas and as far east as Rolla, Missouri. Then, from mid-1863 until the end of the war, four companies, including Porter's, permanently manned "picket posts" at key river or creek crossings in Vernon County, Missouri.

Thus the journal was found to be packed with tantalizing references to places and people still familiar to modern Vernon Countians and others 130 years after. Clearly it was an important primary source, bound to be of growing interest to historians and genealogists. But just as obviously, it fairly cried out for interpretation. Many of the names Porter mentions are no more than names; the substance behind them either has already faded or is fading fast. The present editor began to fancy he might be the one person still around who could make sense of some of Porter's local references. To annotate the journal and see it into print began to loom as a daunting personal duty.

Vernon County had the unenviable fate of being pro-Confederate territory sandwiched between two pro-Union territories: on one side Kansas, with its legacy of anti-Missouri grudges left over from the Border Wars of the 1850s; on the other the often pro-Union and always contrary Missouri hill counties. Federal communication lines between their strong points of Fort Scott in Kansas and Osceola and Springfield in Missouri necessarily passed through Vernon County.

When the regular Confederate forces gave up Missouri in early 1862 many men stayed behind or soon slipped back, behind the Federal lines, hoping to protect their homes and families from the Kansas Jayhawkers, who were using the war to raid and pillage and settle old scores left over from the bitter 1850s. Such irregulars, guerrillas, or partisans drew a measure of legitimation from the Confederate Partisan Ranger Act of April 21, 1862, and experts on military law held irregulars to be entitled to at least some rights as soldiers; but most Federals saw them as outlaws, pure and simple. Pro-Union newspapers began scornfully and sarcastically referring to them as "Bushwhackers": an old word that originally meant simply backwoodsmen—Daniel Boone types.

Some Bushwhackers lived fulltime in the "bush" (i.e. timber), migrating south to warmer climes in the winter. Others masqueraded as ordinary citizens by day and came together by night to ply their controversial trade, attacking Federal wagon trains and small troop detachments. Regular Confederate recruiting officers, coming and going almost at will in a country technically occupied by the Federals, also found themselves regarded as Bushwhackers. Muddling matters still more, the irregular guerrilla life inevitably attracted wild, lawless spirits uninterested in any "cause" save personal whim or gain; their doings tended to deteriorate into outright outlawry, bringing disrepute on all guerrillas. Drawing any kind of lines—between regulars and irregulars, between good guerrillas and bad, between friend and foe—was harder in "occupied Missouri" than almost anywhere else during the Civil War, and grew ever harder as time passed. It called for a finesse the troopers of the 3rd Wisconsin—who like most soldiers throughout history tended to see the world in stark, simpleminded moral black and white— clearly did not possess.

The 3rd's job of "keeping back" the Bushwhackers took the form of frequent scouts and patrols, intelligence work to locate the enemy, and raids on their camps. The job also included cultivating and conciliating the local populace, encouraging and protecting those of known Union sympathies—there might not be too many of those, but some of those few were persons of prominence.

Like most Federals, Porter cherished a blanket poor opinion of Bushwhackers. In his eyes they were outlaws to a man, villains without exception, fighting either for illicit gain or just to indulge their fiendish penchant for indiscriminate violence. They delighted in making war on women and children, as he tells it, and shrank from standing up to their equals.

Porter's ludicrous bias, however, comes across mostly as background, something taken for granted and never made explicit. Seemingly little interested in politics, he never offers a defense or systematic exposition of his opinions. There is a perfunctory tone even to his fiercest words for the foe—those minions of "his Satanic Majesty," those "cowardly, thieving devils," "carrying on their nefarious business." He can hardly bring them up at all, it seems, without an infernal allusion. Out-of-patience with the insect pests and other discomforts of a Missouri summer, he at last disgustedly dubs the whole region "the devil's dominions."

It is a bit of a strain for a descendant of "his Satanic Majesty's minions," of those "cowardly, thieving devils," to forgive Porter his mindless righteousness. Nowhere, it seems, is he struck by the grotesque anomaly—armed strangers from the far North riding roughshod over Missouri under cover of martial law, damning as devils those Missourians who dare, by their lights, stand up for their homes and loved ones, routinely lining them up by the roadside and shooting them down like vermin. How would he have felt, one cannot help wondering, if it had been Missourians dishing out the grim courtesy up in Wisconsin?

His accounts of skirmishes with the Bushwhackers are a bit too onesided to compel complete conviction. The noble Union soldiers, as he puts it, are always badly outnumbered, yet they triumph handily over the dastardly, cowardly Rebels. Rebel bullets never take effect, while every Federal bullet finds its mark. Every contest brings in a well-documented haul of Rebel horses, saddles, and guns. Federal losses, on the other hand—e.g. 27 horses and men on September 24, 1862—rate but the barest mention. Porter manages to glide nimbly and hastily over incidents from which the Federals emerge with less than fulsome martial glory, and seems to devote more space to ferocious threats than to their carrying out. That the Bushwhackers actually make war on women and children is asserted and deplored no end; but when Federal fire wounds a child, on April 5, 1865—oh well, *c'est la guerre!*

After taking up their "picket posts" in mid-1863, the 3rd Wisconsin troopers continued their scouts and their skirmishes with the guerrillas, but inevitably settled into an uneventful or at least unmilitary routine. "With much dancing and flirting," as the local chronicler gibes, "and but little of marching and fighting, the time of the soldiers passed pleasantly, in time they became domesticated, so to speak, mingling freely with the citizens, and some of them found wives for themselves among the 'Rebel' families of the county." "They made occasional scoutings through the country, merely enough to be enjoyable, and sometimes they had a skirmish, only of such frequency, however, as to remind them of their calling." Porter (like fellow Wisconsin trooper Sergeant James P. Mallery, whose 1864 diary was published in 1988) paints pretty much the same picture. The occupiers had not been long on the ground, it is obvious, before they were spending at least as much time and nervous energy chasing and courting the Rebel girls as chasing and battling the Rebel boys.

With so many eligible males either dead or away in the Confederate army, the country was full of lonely young ladies bound to be impressed—politics aside—by the sudden turning-up of an abundance of equally lonely young soldiers. The neighborhood, as

Porter makes plain, had become a country of widows—"the widow Sample," "the widow Redfield," "the widow Woodruff"—all by no means elderly. And still-intact families were overstocked with nubile daughters and other female dependents. The household of Josiah Austin at Balltown (Little Osage), for instance, boasted four eligibles—*all four* of whom would marry 3rd Wisconsin troopers! Venus was in the ascendant, clearly, not Mars.

Only one or two 3rd Wisconsinites were killed in action in Vernon County, but some nine or ten yielded their freedom to matrimony-minded "lady Bushwhackers." (Although many actually were from pro-Union, not "Rebel," families, clearly all were adept at this kind of "bushwhacking"!) Among them was Porter himself. The diarist paid court to a number of ladies, both at Balltown and near Deerfield, before finding himself focusing his attentions on "Bettie," "the widow Rowntree," daughter of one Isaac Evans. It has proved impossible, so far, to identify positively either the Evans or the Rowntree families from the spotty census of 1860, though we learn that Bettie's sister Mary, or Mollie, who married the well-known Jackson County farmer John Scruggs, was born in Garrard County, Kentucky, in 1838.

Porter and Bettie were married at Wyandotte (Kansas City), Kansas, on December 4, 1864, near the end of his term of service. He took her and her daughter Mollie with him back to Baraboo, Wisconsin, where unfortunately record of them disappears.

One or more of the troopers and their wives, however, either settled here at once or shortly returned. For example, Lewis P. Harris and his new wife, the former Mary Jane Wilson (who had been living in the Balltown home of Dr. Leonard Dodge, presumably due to the early death of her parents), settled in the Deerfield area, where they still have descendants.

The first months of Porter's journal, covering his service in the East, were omitted from this rendition, both because it seems less readable and informative and because the editor-annotator lacked the competence to deal with it, as well as the patience to await a competent collaborator. The prime concern was to make available to those to whom it would be of most interest, without undue delay, a basically "Western" Civil War document.

Of the portions of the journal offered here, the only omissions (denoted either by explicit mention or by ellipses) are repetitive remarks about the weather and similar trivia. Only enough of these are included to give the flavor of the whole—it seemed pointless to repeat over and over such meticulous, conscientious mentions as "Today I made out my payrolls," etc. Porter's prose is given substantially as he wrote it, orthographic idiosyncracies and all, with interpretation offered only where glaringly called for. The index is by day rather than page. Of some of the more frequent references (e.g. Fort Scott, Kansas), only the most significant are included in the index.

Thanks are due, and are hereby sincerely tendered, to all those involved in bringing the effort to fruition, already cited: to Herb and the late Gordon Davis, the journal's discoverers; to the State Historical Society of Wisconsin, who made the original available; and to Arnold Schofield and his staff at the Fort Scott National Historic Site, who provided the transcript.

The editor also thanks: Fred L. Lee, Kansas City; Keith I. Daleen, Sedalia; Richard L. Norton, Springfield; Robert S. Barrows, Rochester N. Y.; Montgomery and Bridget Fitzwater, Mound City, Kan.; Thomas Goodrich, Topeka, Kan.; Shirley Harris Park, Tulsa, Okla.; as well as staffers of the Kansas State Historical Society and the State Historical Society of Missouri, especially (of the latter) Executive Director Dr. James Goodrich. All provided invaluable research aid and/or suggestions.

❦ 1862 ❦

We join Porter and the regiment on their way overland south from Fort Leavenworth, on the Missouri River, to Fort Scott, in central southeast Kansas.

Monday, June 16. This morning at 5 O'clock we continued our journey. We passed a few farms today. More timber today than seen on our journey. This forenoon cool and cloudy. At 11 O'clock A.M. we camped 1½ miles north of Fort Scott, Kans. We marched 10 miles today. We put up our tents for the first time since we left Leavenworth. Rain this evening.

Tuesday, June 17. This morning at 6 O'clock our Battalion came out on Dress parade, after which we had a general wash day, for our cloths [sic] were full of dust from our recent march. We had some rain last night and today quite hot.

Wednesday, June 18. There was nothing unusual in camp this forenoon. After dinner we packed tents and baggage and moved to Fort Scott and located our camp. Henry Mankee[1] a member of my company was taken sick and sent to the hospital. We got our camp fixed up in good shape. Major [Benjamin] Henning[2] was assigned to the command of the fort and Provost Marshall taking command on arriving. . . .

1. Private Henry Manke, Dellona, Wis., died of disease on June 26.

2. Major Benjamin S. Henning, Oshkosh, Wis., commanded the Second Battalion of the Regiment.

1862 - 2

Thursday, June 19. This forward [sic] I was engaged fixing my tent more convenient and providing myself with a rustic bedstead composed of forked sticks drove in the ground and poles laid on then bark was wove across for bottom. Afternoon, I spent in the Fort which was located on the south side of Marmaton river.[1] The day quite hot.

1. The Marmaton River flows generally east through Bourbon County, Kan., into Missouri where it joins the Osage, having passed just north of Fort Scott. The fort, now restored as a National Historic Site, overlooks the river from a high bluff.

Friday, June 20. Company "C" left camp this morning to be gone eight days on a scout in the vicinity of Mine Creek.[1] Two confederates were brought in from Cedar County, Mo.,[2] and was confined in the "Bastillion" of the Fort. I did not learn of any farther news to note down. The day was pleasant.

1. Mine Creek flows northeastward through southern Linn County, Kan., some 30 miles north of Fort Scott, emptying into the Marais des Cygnes River.
2. Cedar County, Mo., begins 35 miles east of Fort Scott.

For four days Porter recorded only routine matters. "Card and ball playing seems to be the past time in camp." "Mosquitoes and flies were my constant companions in camp."

Wednesday, June 25. After breakfast I walked down to the Blacksmith shop, my attention being attracted there by soldiers conducting thirteen prisoners from the guard-house to that point. I found on my arrival that the smiths were putting shackles upon the ankles of the prisoners. They seemed to be quite jolly and sported over their new acquisitions of government jewelry. They was immediately sent to Fort Leavenworth for final trial. . . .

Thursday, June 26. This morning there was a detail of fifty men of our Company under command of Lieut. W. J. Plows[1]—ordered to Montevallo, Mo.[2] about forty miles distant to reconnoiter for the enemy. I accompanied the scouting party on this expedition. We started at 8 O'clock A.M. from camp and soon crossed the Missouri line. We enjoyed this our first chance for a little excitement. During the afternoon we came upon a party at a house who were dancing, the men looked suspicious, but our commander suffered them to continue the dance and we continued on our way. We camped for the night at 10½ O'clock P.M. . . .

1. First Lieutenant William J. Plows, Milwaukee, Wis., promoted from Battalion Sergeant Major May 1.

2. "Old" Montevallo, over a mile west of the modern community, between McCarty and Mill creeks, had been burned by two companies of the First Iowa Cavalry on April 14, after an attack on them in the town by local Confederates.

Friday, June 27. This morning at 2 O'clock we was again on our way. We scouted the woods during the day and came out to the little town of Montevallo where we procured refreshments, and some whiskey from a still house near by. We found everything quiet here, no business astir here, a dilapidated place and the few remaining citizens presented a forlorn condition. We soon took our departure and scouted the country during the day, at about dark the company camped. I was ordered to take a part of the company and go to a point three miles distant to arrest some Jayhawkers or Bushwhackers.[1] On my arrival I discovered our man trying to escape when 8 or 9 shots were fired without harm and the man soon surrendered, we found he was not the man we wanted and we turned him loose. Our game was not to be found, so we returned to camp. The day hot.

1. Porter fails to keep the useful distinction between Jayhawkers (usually Unionist Kansans) and Bushwhackers (usually Confederate Missourians); like many other regulars he seemingly regarded both as mere outlaws.

Saturday, June 28. After a scant breakfast we turned our course towards Fort Scott. After a hot march we arrived at camp in the Fort at 5 O'clock P.M. Soon after our arrival a heavy storm came upon us accompanied by rain, hail, and wind, which soon blew our tents down leaving us exposed to rain and the merciless pelting of hail. After the storm abated we set to work putting up tents again and retired in wet clothes for the night.

Sunday, June 29. This morning I learned that Henry Manke who was sent to the Hospital[1] on our first arrival at the Fort died on the 26th inst. and was buried in the Military Cemetery[2] at Fort Scott, Kansas where our company erected a suitable head stone to his memory. We also learned that Sergt. Clayhorn K. Robinson[3] of our Co. died on the 18th inst. at his home, Ironton, Wis. George Norris[4] of our Co. deserted today taking horse and equipments. Today was warm and pleasant.

1. The fort hospital building has been restored, or reconstructed, and houses the National Historic Site headquarters.

2. National Cemetery No. 1, the nation's oldest, is located at the southeast edge of the town.

3. Sergeant Claghorn K. Robinson, Ironton, Wis., died at his home of unspecified disease.

4. Private George Norris, St. Louis, Mo., enlisted April 18, deserted officially on July 1.

Monday, June 30. Today there was nothing of interest with us. I spent a part of the day looking over different points about the fort and government buildings which I found to be not as extensive as those of Leavenworth. There was six 24 & 32 pounder Siege guns constituting the armament of the Fort, and the buildings were in a bad condition. I returned to camp in due time for evening Roll Call. . . .

Tuesday, July 1. There was nothing interesting with us today all hands seem to be prostrated with laziness as the weather was very hot today. In my rambles today about town I came upon a citizen by name of Clark who lived near my fathers in my boyhood, he kept a restaurant and saloon here. He was of a jolly turn and to my liking. I took dinner with him and then we talked over of bygone days. I took leave of him with an invitation to again make him a visit.

Wednesday, July 2. The day being extremely hot our camp presented a mass of inactive humanity, never did laziness reign supreme to so great an extent as in our camp. Eat and sleep seems to be the order of the day and I doubted if the approach of an enemy would arouse the men to action. I hope soon to take a forward move for new fields of labor as our duties seem to be too few at present.

Thursday, July 3. Today was spent as usual. I did not learn of anything from the army at other point of late. Likely they are in our situation. We seem to be an isolated number stationed here to guard the lives of money sharks, Saloon keepers and citizens. . . .

Friday, July 4. Today was ushered in by the usual salute of guns from the Fort in honor of our National Independence. Well, our camp seemed to show a more busy appearance as the heavy boom of the canon [sic] had the effect of shaking off the lethargy of camp preparatory to the festivities of the day.

The saloons commenced business with a fair prospect of a bountiful haul of cash. A large dance was in progress in the Fort at an early hour this evening, which I attended. There was other parties of the kind in the vicinity which gave ample room for all who desired to participate. We had a pleasant time today and dancing continued to be in full attendance at a late hour of the night. The weather was extremely hot. I did not learn of any rows or accidents in the Fort today.

Saturday, July 5. This morning a drowsy set made their appearance at Roll call. My belief is, that the boys are about to relapse into their former habits, as I am frequently compelled to resort to harsh methods to compel the men to perform the necessary duties required of them. The day was extremely hot.

Sunday, July 6. Today was another hot one, and a general cessation of business anymore than necessary to run the military machinery of the Fort and camp. I busied myself writing to friends today.

Monday, July 7. Today the monotony of camp continues as usual. How long oh Lord must this continue is the yawning exclamation heard in camp. Terrible hot today.

For ten days Porter wrote only of the weather and boredom.

Wednesday, July 16. I had the satisfaction of being detailed to take charge of the guard who guarded prisoners at the Guard House. We have one noted prisoner by the name of Henry Taylor,[1] late Sheriff of Vernon Co., Mo. and at the time of his capture was Captain of a Bushwhacking party. I had a conversation with him and found him a man of great ability, he claimed to have a commission in the Confederate Service. The day was quite pleasant.

1. William Henry Taylor, 28, in 1860 resided in the City Hotel in Nevada and called himself a merchant. Elected sheriff that fall, he resigned in early 1861 to become quartermaster of the Seventh Cavalry Regiment, Eighth Division, Missouri State Guard. After the disbanding of the State Guard, following Pea Ridge, he came back to his home area around Montevallo to recruit. A speech by Colonel John T. Coffee in Montevallo in early April, 1862, led to the recruitment of some 70 area men for Taylor's company. Taylor was captured on April 14 while breakfasting at a house southeast of Montevallo by Second Iowa Cavalrymen on their way to the town. Paroled and living in Nevada City when it was burned by Federal militia a year later, Taylor continued to pursue his bushwhacking activites. After the war he was reelected sheriff. He was also Montevallo's postmaster.

Thursday, July 17. Was relieved from guard duty this morning. I went to camp and found everything quiet but in some tents could be found a "Rip Van Winkle" sleeper. The day quite pleasant.

Friday, July 18. Today the usual camp duties was performed then we resumed the accustomed lazy life of camp which if continued will produce a demoralizing effect upon our boys. The weather is becoming hot.

Saturday, July 19. Today we was blessed with more rain which cooled the air and made us happy. The boys who was off duty was engaged in various pursuits such as letter writing, card playing, etc.

Sunday, July 20. This morning was balmy but as the day advances the atmosphere becomes hot. We have no minister to direct our course to that country where but one rebellion is said to have existed and that was inaugurated by the Devil. So we try to pass the time as best we can. I learn that another scouting party will be sent out soon.

Monday, July 21. This morning I was ordered to detail twentyfive men of my Company and join other detailed from the Battalion and proceed on a scout in Missouri. We started on our trip at an early hour and took an eastward course, we marched about 25 miles and camped about dark near Montevallo. We took supper then stationed the necessary guard and laid down for the night nothing worthy of note transpired today.

Tuesday, July 22. This morning Capt. [Theodore] Conkey[1] our commander had us up as soon as day dawned and as soon as we fed our horses we partook of our breakfast and soon we was on our way to Montevallo passed on through town a short distance and encountered a party of Bushwhackers, when a lively fight ensued in which three of their number was sent to the happy hunting ground, and four of their horses and equipments fell to us as trophys of victory, the remaining number escaped. We sustained no injury or loss. Day hot. We took a north course till night when we camped.

1. Theodore Conkey, Appleton, Wis., captain of Co. I.

Wednesday, July 23. This morning we was early on the move, over prairies and through timber, all anxious for a fight. We could not find any game today or learn of any being in that part of the country. So we headed for Fort Scott, arrived in camp at 8 O'clock P.M. The day very hot.

Thursday, July 24. This morning we came forth from our tents well rested. We hope soon to take another scout. This afternoon we had another shower but not of long duration. All quiet in camp.

Friday, July 25. The same duties being performed in camp as usual this morning, the camp soon put on the same monotonous aspect as usual. I took a stroll about the fortifications this afternoon and found others there when we joined in a few jokes and anecdotes to the enjoyment of the party. The day hot.

Saturday, July 26. We are tormented by mosquitoes and a species of bug, these bugs run in our ears and keep up a constant scrabble until drowned out and occasionally a snake takes up lodging with us and a lively scene may be witnessed in the morning. The day passed off as usual. Very hot today.

Sunday, July 27. We are in tolerable good health but few on sick list, we hardly recognize a Sunday when it comes, as the same duties fall to us as other days, no sound of church bell here. I presume this place is intended for fitting men for war and not for heaven as no provision seem to have been made for the latter. The day passed away as usual. Very hot today.

Monday, July 28. This day I took a stroll around the government building and formed some new acquaintances. I met with two young ladies with whom I spent a pleasant hour, they live close by the fort. Thus I spent the day though quite hot.

Tuesday, July 29. Today the accustomed duties of camp having been accomplished the boys turned out in force for a cloths [sic] washing. The Marmaton river for wash tub and large flat rocks for wash boards, with a plenty of soap the job was soon accomplished when dry they are smoothed with the hands. Thus the day was spent.

Wednesday, July 30. We had a camp cleaning today so as to keep healthy. This evening our camp presented a more tidy appearance and the boys looked more cheerful. Tonight we had some good songs and violin music by some of the boys. Day quite pleasant.

Thursday, July 31. Today I spent in camp reading some papers I borrowed, they was full of news from our Potomac Army and of course we was quite anxious to learn what they was doing and if any reliability can be placed in the reports. I think our boys there, have a gigantic undertaking before them.

Friday, August 1. Today everything in camp seemed to have thrown off its lazy attire and put on a more cheerful aspect the boys were regulating their habitations and by orders from their officers they cleaned up arms and accouterments. I think from appearance that we are soon to find enough to keep us on the move. The weather is some pleasanter.

Saturday, August 2. The usual duties of the morning having been performed, such as guard mounting, and our horses fed and watered, and being at liberty I procured a dime Novel and spent the day perusing its pages. Nothing unusual transpired with us today. The day dry and quite hot.

Sunday, August 3. The morning our company and two others of our Battalion left camp and took a westerly course in Kansas through Marmaton[1] the county seat of Bourbon County, we continued our course through some fine country and camped at 4 O'clock P.M. on a platoon [plateau?] near a creek. Day pleasant.

1. Still a crossroads community in central Bourbon County, between Fort Scott and Redfield (Section 31, T 25 S, R 23-24 E); before devastation in the war a considerable village, briefly the county seat.

Monday, August 4. This morning early a dispatch came ordering us to return to Fort Scott without delay. We saddled up and started immediately without breakfast. We arrived in the Fort at 9 O'clock A.M. and took breakfast. Immediately my Company and Co. "C" in Capt. [Edward] Stevens[1] commanding and Co. "M", Capt. [Henry] Rouse[2] commanding started on an expedition in Missouri, our march was very rapid reaching Montevallo we encountered a force of enemy numbering 800 our force was about 225. We reconnoitered their position and found them surrounding us, after consultation the officers decided to retreat as our position was precarious. We commenced an orderly retreat, but soon the whole outfit was making a precipitate retreat and the enemy in full pursuit. We took two prisoners and the enemy captured our Surgeon and two 6 mule teams and wagons our retreat extended fifteen miles.

1. Edward R. Stevens, Kingston, Wis., Captain of Company C.
2. Henry F. Rouse, Mazomanie, Wis., Captain of Company M.

Tuesday, August 5. We will continue to give a farther account of our retreat of yesterday. Our course was south from Montevallo to a point called Hog-eye[1] over a large prairie and we not only went at a moderate pace, but went at a devilish fast speed, every one seemed to consider a good retreat preferably [sic] to capture. One of our prisoners horse fell throwing him off and breaking his neck, as was supposed, not a stop was made to investigate. We stopped at Hog-eye and collected our scattered forces, and we partook of a scant ration then turned our course toward Fort Scott and we traveled all night, this morning we arrived at camp in the Fort. Our troops looked sadly dilapidated and swearing that this was the first and last retreat they should make that fighting was preferable. We spent the day resting ourselves and jaded horses. Day pleasant.

1. A former settlement in SE Sec. 5, Milford Twp., Barton County. Hog-eye is sometimes termed an early nickname for Nevada, because "hogs had a wallow in the center of the settlement."—Bernice Johnson, *Place-names in Six of the West Central Counties of Missouri*, master's thesis, University of Missouri, 1933, quoting Andy J. King. Bernice Johnson Teel admitted to the present writer that there was no corroboration. Robert L. Ramsey (*Our Storehouse of Missouri Place Names*, Columbia, 1973) apparently only picked up her entry.

Wednesday, August 6. This morning we came forth from our couch some refreshed but lame from the furious ride we took. Well, I suppose such is the fortunes of war, but my experience in this instance is, I have no desire for a repetition of the mixture in my rations. Some of the boys came in camp today whose horses gave out on the retreat, some are still missing. Day hot.

Thursday, August 7. This evening Chas. Swift[1] came in camp. He was a member of my Co. His horse fell dead on retreat and he concealed himself in the grass till a chance presented its self for escape when he took a course for camp, he took sick and lay in the woods one day and night without food or water. . . .

1. Charles Swift, Cazenovia, Wis., corporal, afterwards commissary sergeant; discharged for disability Nov. 30, 1864.

Friday, August 8. We continue in camp are improving in condition. There seems to be a desire among the boys to try the "Johnnies" again when they are of the opinion that a skedaddle will fall to the lot of the enemy. There is some talk of moving camp to a healthier locality. The weather is hot and dusty.

Saturday, August 9. After breakfast we the 2nd Battalion packed tents and camp equipage and moved east of Fort Scott about three miles and located. We was busy nearly all day putting our camp in order. The surroundings are much more pleasant than those of our former camp. We had a pleasant day.

Sunday, August 10. We spent the day pleasant in camp and made some improvements for comfort. This evening our Surgeon B. O. Reynolds[1] who was captured, came in camp, having escaped from the enemy near Carthage, Mo.[2] Nothing more transpired with us of interest. The day cool and pleasant.

1. Benoni O. Reynolds, Elkhorn, Wis., regimental surgeon.
2. Seat of Jasper County, Mo., 50 miles south; a strongly Confederate area, as Porter confirms on August 20.

Monday, August 11. The boys who was off duty was washing and mending their clothes today. The day was warm and pleasant. Company drills and

Dress parades seem to be a past luxury, as our companies seem to be proficient for service.

Tuesday, August 12. Reports came in camp today that a large confederate force are on their way from Arkansas, but can not find out the direction they are going. I learn that we are to be in readiness for a move at any moment. All are anxious to hear the word "Forward." Troops are arriving this evening in the Fort, so a fight is soon to take place undoubtedly.

Wednesday, August 13. This morning at a little past midnight our Company and Capt. Conkeys Company joined a force of 1500 more troops and started on an expedition in Missouri. We took an easterly course, at 8 O'clock A.M. we halted for breakfast, after which we resumed our onward course in a southeasterly direction moving slowly on our way, the day cool, night find us on our way, no supper but some "Hard tack" and raw bacon from our haversacks satisfy hunger to some extent. On, on we go during the night, halting occasionally for our wagons to come up.

Thursday, August 14. This morning found us continuing on our way having marched all night making but slow headway our train of wagons seem to impede our progress. We stopped a short time to feed our horses, our ration wagons did not reach us, so we was minus breakfast, we was soon ordered forward, continued our way until 2 O'clock P.M. when we halted to graze our horses and get our dinner, here we remained till 6 O'clock P.M. where the command was again moving forward till 11 O'clock P.M. we camped for the night 15 miles southwest from the town of Montevallo, Mo. The day cool but dusty.

Friday, August 15. This morning we had breakfast early, and when ready to move, a dispatch arrived ordering us to turn our course northward as the enemy we was in pursuit of was fast moving in that direction. We began a rapid move forward at 8 O'clock A.M. and we hurried until 3 O'clock P.M. when we halted for supper and feed our horses. Col. [W. F.] Cloud[1] of 2nd Kans. Cavalry commanding our Cavalry. At 6 O'clock P.M. we felt rested and a forward move again commenced. Night found us journeying over prairies and rocky hills and timber country, at 11 O'clock P.M. we camp for the night.

1. Colonel W. F. Cloud, commanding 2nd Kansas Cavalry Regiment; said to have saved the Vernon County public records after their return to Fort Scott from Arkansas in 1865.

Saturday, August 16. This morning the boys was foraging early, the result being a sumptuous breakfast of chickens, beef and mutton. We saddled up and at 8 O'clock A.M. we was again on our way. Soon crossing the Osage river[1] going a short distance we halted to await further orders. We remained thus until 5 O'clock P.M. when we was again ordered forward continued our journey over some terrible rough country until 1 O'clock in the night when we halted.

1. The major stream of west central Missouri, the Osage proper is formed by the junction of the Marais des Cygnes and Marmaton-Little Osage some 7 miles east of Rich Hill, Mo.; here it separates Bates and Vernon counties.

Sunday, August 17. This morning at 2 O'clock we was on the move again at 7 O'clock in the morning we arrived at Kingsvilla[1] and took breakfast. It rained all last night. We found Genl. [James] Blunts[2] forces here, and was informed that a heavy battle was fought at Lone Jack[3] yesterday, both sides claiming the victory, but the enemy took the back track during last night. After breakfast we started in pursuit of the enemy, the rain continued to fall during the day. Our force consists of Cavalry, Infantry, and Artillery. The infantry are hauled in mule wagons to move with more rapidity. We start at 9 O'clock A.M. leaving Genl. Blunt at Rose Hill.[4] We made a forced march today and took some stragglers prisoner. Camped at 7 O'clock P.M.

1. Kingsville, in western Johnson County, Mo.

2. A rabid Abolitionist, James G. Blunt was commissioned brigadier general April 8, 1862; on May 5 appointed commander of the Department of Kansas, headquartered at Paola; promoted major general Nov. 29.

3. The Battle of Lone Jack, in Jackson County, Mo., in which the Vernon County Confederates took part, is usually seen as a Confederate victory.

4. A community in extreme southwest Johnson County, Mo., reportedly burned to the ground by Jayhawkers in 1863.

Monday, August 18. Our ration wagon could not reach us last eve, so the Cavalry boys provided themselves with meal and a few tin kettles, so our breakfast consists of boiled meal, we eat it out of corn shucks, at 4 O'clock A.M. We the cavalry took the lead and the other troops following my company was on the advance today, and indications were that the enemy were not far ahead, so we kept flankers on each side of the road. We kept on a gallop a great part of the time, I was on the left flank and passing through a field we came in sight of a squad of the enemy leaving a house at a lively rate. We came to the house and found a large kettle of roasting ears on a fire already cooked which we soon took in and went our way. At about 2 O'clock P.M. we came upon the enemy 4500 strong on the south of the Osage river at Taborville.[1] Our infantry and Artillery was fifteen miles in our rear, and our cavalry force numbered 600 Col. Cloud commanding. We had traveled 50 miles since morning and not liking to loose [sic] our game, the gallant Colonel gave orders for us to attack the enemy who was drawn up in battle array. We made a furious charge the enemy fired a volley at us without effect, then retreated while we pursued and kept up a constant firing, and capturing some prisoners, after retreating a mile they made another stand and we soon routed them again and a running fight for seven miles was the result at about dark we found the enemy scattered and in full retreat. So we camped for the night without loss of a man. Our horses was too tired to continue farther pursuit. We learn that the enemy lost ten killed and many wounded. We retired without supper as sleep was preferable with us. The day was warm and dusty.

1. Taberville, on the Osage River in western St. Clair County.

Tuesday, August 19. This morning at an early hour our camp was making haste to give the Johnies another uneasy day of it. We eat our scanty breakfast of boiled meal and at the hour of 7 O'clock the entire command was again moving southward. At 3 O'clock P.M. we passed through Montevalo, continued a south course until 9 O'clock P.M. when we camped. No enemy seen today. We are of the opinion that our company is not very desirable to them. We retire for the night without supper. The day quite pleasant.

Wednesday, August 20. This morning after our Mush was devoured but partially appeasing our hunger, we was in our saddles at 5½ O'clock and on the move. At 7 O'clock A.M. we passed Lamar the county seat of Barton Co. A citizen of the place by name of Martin Voscar[1] joined us and we soon found he once resided in Baraboo, Wis. He seemed to be full of joy at finding many old acquaintances in my Company.[2] So he continued with us today. At 3 O'clock P.M. we crossed Spring River,[3] after marching a half hour we arrived at Carthage, the county seat of Jasper Co., Mo. We all made a raid on the citizens for the purpose of getting supper and I am confident that when our appetites were satisfied a hungry person would meet with poor success in the breakfast line next morning. The citizens were secessionists. Here we camped for the night. No enemy seen today. Day hot.

1. Unidentified.

2. 70 officers and men in Company F called Baraboo their hometown.

3. Spring River flows roughly east to west through Jasper County.

Thursday, August 21. We got up early and soon received a Dispatch from Genl. [John B.] Sanbourn[1] that he was in pursuit of the enemy and would relieve us of farther pursuit. At 11 O'clock A.M. we saddled our horses and marched north 8 miles and camped near a beautiful spring. I procured supper at a house of a Union family. Our supper consisted of biscuit & butter, chicken pie and good coffee. Here we camped for the night. Day was hot.

1. Brigadier General John B. Sanborn commanded a brigade of the Provisional Enrolled Missouri Militia (Federal) at Springfield.

Friday, August 22. We spent the day procuring rations and resting our horses. Our ration wagon has returned to Fort Scott with the infantry & Artillery. So we are obliged to subsist as best we can. Day hot.

Saturday, August 23. This morning at 7 O'clock A.M. we was again in the saddle and on the road for Fort Scott. The 6th Kansas Cavalry took the advance. Soon after starting they came upon a force of 800 or 1000 Confederates under the command of Genl. Cockran,[1] we cut them off and pursued them northward to Coon Creek[2] where the advance engaged them at about noon. We was soon up to assist the 6th Kansas who was hotly engaged losing 5 killed & 13 wounded. Two more Companies of the 6th came up and was soon engaged, losing 3 Corporals killed. The 3rd Wis. Cav. luckily met with no accidents. We soon had the enemy scattered and in full retreat. We gathered up our dead and wounded and started for Lamar, arriving at 7 O'clock P.M. and camped. Our citizen friend Voscar invited me to his home where his amiable wife set us good supper which we soon appropriated to our rapacious appetites after which we repaired to the Hotel where the surgeons were attending to our wounded comrades after spending some little time there I went to camp and turned in for the night. The day was warm and pleasant.

1. Perhaps Francis Marion Cockrell, Captain Co. G 3rd Infantry Regiment, Missouri State Guard, afterwards Brigadier General CSA.

2. Coon Creek rises in northeast Jasper County and flows west into the North or Muddy Fork of Spring River.

Sunday, August 24. At 7 O'clock this morning we was again on the move towards Fort Scott. I understand that the dead were buried by their comrades during the night. After we had moved out on the road about two miles, we halted for the ambulances and baggage wagons to join us at 10 O'clock A.M. We then started on our course and at sunset we halted to rest the wounded. At 8 O'clock P.M. we started on our way. At midnight we arrived in camp at Fort Scott. Ludger

Phoenix[1] had his thumb shot to pieces by accidental discharge of carbine when dismounting from his horse. Day hot.

1. Private Ledger Phoenix, Cazenovia, Wis., discharged April 1, 1863, with disability.

Monday, August 25. Today we spent eating and sleeping to mend our worn out bodies, for we have made up our minds that Uncle Sam has got work for us to do, and our days of lounging in camp are luxuries we are to dispense with in the future. So we are trying to make up for loss of sleep and rations. Today hot.

Tuesday, August 26. Today I felt rested so I commenced the task of making up my Company Muster and Pay Rolls. I learn that Geo. Richards[1] a member of my company died at the Hospital on the 24th day of this month. I also learned that Arnold Pratt[2] was dead, he was a member of my Co. but was detailed to drive a mule team. The day hot.

1. Porter later corrects this report. Private George Richards, Baraboo, Wis., did not die till Sept. 11, of disease.

2. Private Arnold Pratt, Baraboo, Wis., did not die at all, but was discharged with disability on Nov. 22.

For nine days Porter wrote only of the weather, boredom in camp, and making out the company payrolls.

Friday, September 5. Our camp is located one mile east of Fort Scott. I went to the Fort this morning in company with Moris F. Waite[1] a member of my Co. who was going to Wisconsin to recruit for the company. I spent the day in the Fort. The troops here at present seem to be enjoying quite a degree of inactivity. The day quite hot.

1. Morris E. Waite, Baraboo, Wis., quartermaster sergeant, afterwards commissary sergeant; discharged with disability April 29, 1864.

Saturday, September 6. This morning a rain storm came and continued through the day. At noon my Company Captains Conkey and Rousis Companies with 100 wagons started out on a foraging expedition in Missouri. At 8 O'clock P.M. we camped at Balltown[1] on the Osage[2] river 22 miles north east from Fort Scott. Our supper consisted of fried chickens, mutton, hardbread and honey.

1. Properly Little Osage, west of present Horton, Mo.
2. Properly the Little Osage River.

Sunday, September 7. This morning at 8 O'clock we was again on the move in a northerly course, crossing the Osage river soon after starting. At noon we passed through Papinsville,[1] a small town, but the best portion of the town had been burnt by Kansas troops by order of Jim Lane,[2] so said. After a mile farther on the road we came upon plenty of corn and filled our wagons. While there we saw about 100 troops at quite a distance crossing a prairie, whom we took to be

Confederates. At 2 O'clock P.M. we started back on our road and we camped at the place we did last night. Day hot. *(On the 8th the party returned uneventfully to Fort Scott and there rested quietly on the 9th.)*

1. Papinsville, or Papinville, lies on the Marais des Cygnes (the Big Osage) River in southeast Bates County; burned Dec. 8, 1861, by Maj. James M. Williams, of James Montgomery's Regiment, part of Lane's force. See *The Richard Ely Selden, Jr., Letters of 1866,* Robert S. Barrows, ed., Rochester, N.Y., 1997.

2. James H. Lane, Brigadier General of his own "Kansas Legion" or "Brigade," dismissed as a jayhawking "rabble" even by Unionists, mustered into Federal service April 8, 1862.

Wednesday, September 10. This morning we the above Companies was detailed to proceed on another foraging expedition. At 8 O'clock A.M. we started out for Missouri. We took an east course. At 3 P.M. we passed through a small but beautiful town.[1] I did not learn the name. It was nearly deserted. At 6 O'clock P.M. we camped a distance of 24 miles from Fort Scott, our journey was over some fine country today. We had a fine supper as usual on all foraging expeditions. The day was rainy which made our trip rather a disagreeable one. We sleep in wet clothes tonight.

1. This hardly sounds like Nevada City (modern Nevada), though no alternative readily comes to mind.

Thursday, September 11. This morning at 8 O'clock we started on our way after we had gone three miles we found corn enough to load our wagons 125 in number. At 2 O'clock P.M. we started on our road back we took some horses today from those who were not friendly to our cause. We camped near where we camped last night. This forenoon was rainy. Afternoon cloudy and cool, wind northwest.

Friday, September 12. This morning early we had breakfast after a cold nights sleep on the ground. Some frost last night at 6 O'clock A.M. we was again on the road to Fort Scott. After we had gone 7 miles we sent the teams forward with a small escort, then we took another direction in search of stock. We captured 452 cattle and 60 sheep then we returned to where we left our wagons and camps. This forenoon cloudy and cool. Afternoon warm & pleasant.

Saturday, September 13. This morning at 9 O'clock we started on the road to the Fort we came to a stream called Drywood[1] soon after starting. Our Lieut. W. J. Plows got into a yellow jackets nest here which occasioned a great deal of merriment for all of us, as the Lieut. beat a lively retreat from the little force that assailed him. We soon got our stock over the creek, after we had marched 15 miles we arrived at camp at 2 O'clock P.M. After we had partaken of our dinner we moved camp a half mile on a hill. The day was hot.

1. Big Drywood Creek flows due north, entering the Marmaton River just to the east of present Deerfield, Mo.

Sunday, September 14. We learn this morning that Geo. Richards died on the 11th inst. at the Hospital. I received a letter this morning from Bro. Samuel[1] at Baraboo, Wis. and Bro. Walworth[2] received one from Bro. Albert[3] of the 14th Wis. Infantry at Corinth, Miss. both were well. There was nothing important in camp today. I went to the camp of Augustus Brooks[4] our ambulance driver and spent the evening in card playing with Brooks wife and had a pleasant time. I returned to my quarters in due time. The day very hot. *(The 15th was uneventful.)*

1. Samuel Porter, brother of the diarist.
2. Walworth D. Porter, Baraboo, Wis., another brother of the diarist, corporal in the company, afterwards sergeant.
3. Albert Porter, another brother of the diarist.
4. Pvt. Henry Augustus Brooks, Green Bay, Wis., wagoner.

Tuesday, September 16. This morning I went with my Company out on the Leavenworth road to escort five more Companies of our Regiment to our camp [who] have just arrived from Leavenworth where they had been on duty. Soon after arriving it commenced to rain and continued until some time in the night. At about dark, a young man of Co. "M" was accidentally killed by his revolver which was in the hands of a member of Co. "G" at the time. The accident was lamented by all of us. I did not learn deceased name.[1]

1. Private William S. Closson, Boscobel, Wis.

For four days Porter reported only camp routine.

Sunday, September 21. Another Sunday has come, no sound of church bells greets the ear of mortal here, but instead the fife, drum and bugle is heard from all quarters, not for the purpose of calling us to pay homage, to our maker, but the commands of a Colonel Major the lowest in office a Corporal [sic]. After breakfast we had Dress parade for a change. After returning to our quarters, the same monotony of camp took place, as a frequent exhibition of laziness was every where apparent. Today pleasant.

Monday, September 22. This morning at 10 O'clock we had marching orders which was hailed with delight. Our companies commenced packing tents and equipage and all hands were busy. At 5 O'clock P.M. the whole command was on the move towards Missouri. We marched all night. The day was pleasant.

Tuesday, September 23. This morning at 6 O'clock we halted at Nevada, Mo.[1] the county seat of Vernon County here we took breakfast. This place is destroyed not many houses remain and but one family remain. At 11 O'clock A.M. we took up our march towards Montevalo [sic] Major Henning commanding about two miles from Montevalo, our Company was sent out to reconnoiter the country. We found no enemy so we joined the command at Montevalo at 6 O'clock P.M. and camped. The day was hot.

1. Nevada had been visited by several Jayhawker and other Federal units since the outbreak of the war, but was not

"destroyed" till May 26, 1863. Eyewitness reports from that date speak of a population of from 25 to 150, and from six to a dozen families. Porter's impression is hard to account for.

Wednesday, September 24. This morning a part of our force started out on a foraging expedition and returned camp about dark. A little before sun set Corporals W. D. Porter, J. Wright,[1] and Privates H. H. Rice,[2] J. Riley,[3] and H. Statia[4] were taken prisoners while watering their horses. Their captors were Brice Mayfield[5] and party of bush-whackers. Their sister Miss Mayfield[6] came to our camp and notified us of the capture.[7] Miss Mayfield was retained in camp tonight. The day was warm.

1. Corporal James Wright, Baraboo, Wis.
2. Private Hiram H. Rice, Baraboo, Wis., musician.
3. Private James Riley, Dellona, Wis.
4. Private Hiram Statia, Baraboo, Wis.
5. Brice R. Mayfield and brother John Crawford "Crack" Mayfield, led an active and notorious Bushwhacker band centered on their home area of Dover and Montevallo townships. Both brothers were killed near Neosho, Mo., on Dec. 26, 1862.
6. Ella Mayfield, eldest of the three Mayfield sisters, took up the torch after her brothers' deaths and became widely known as the leading "lady Bushwhacker" of Vernon County.
7. Porter plays down this embarrassing incident. Colonel Charles A. Doubleday, of the 2nd Ohio Cavalry, commanded "Doubleday's Brigade, Department of Missouri," including his own and other regiments, involved in several area actions in 1862. Reportedly on this occasion Doubleday complained that the Mayfields had captured, disarmed, and dismounted 27 of his men, and he sarcastically ordered the commanding officer in the field to come home, "as we have no orders to furnish the Confederate

service with cavalry horses."—Letter of Frank P. Anderson to *Nevada Daily Mail,* Jan. 30, 1894. Ella Mayfield was sent to the enemy camp to offer to trade the captured men for Captain Taylor. The offer being refused, the captives were released after a few days.—*The History of Vernon County, Mo.,* 336.

Thursday, September 25. This morning at 11 O'clock we was again on the move in a north course at 1 O'clock P.M. we camped again. I can't comprehend why we are on the seeming fool trip. . . .

Friday, September 26. At 9 O'clock this morning the command was again on the move in a north direction after a march of two miles we camped on a prairie near timber. We put up tents and afternoon I went with my company and a number of teams for corn and found a supply and returned to camp at dark. The day hot and dusty.

Saturday, September 27. This morning at 9 O'clock I was again on the road with my Company and 20 wagons after corn, we found sufficient to load our wagons and returned to camp at 4 O'clock P.M. Company "C" went out four miles west of Montevalo in search of bushwhackers, they had a skirmish with 20 of them, soon putting them to flight, no loss reported on either side. Day hot.

Sunday, September 28. Early this morning our camp was thrown into excitement by Companies "C" and "M" firing their guns. The balance of the command supposing an attack by the enemy had taken place, was soon in readiness to receive them, but finding it was a false alarm, no little amount of curses was heaped upon Companies "C" and "M" as a heavy rain was falling at the time. This afternoon Company "E" returned to camp and brought in a number of horses captured from Mayfields camp. The day cloudy and cool.

Monday, September 29. There was nothing unusual with us today. We all lay in camp today, enjoying ourselves as well as possible. We have not learned the fate of those who were taken prisoners. I feel quite anxious to know, as my brother was one of the number. This afternoon we was ordered to be ready to return to Fort Scott on the morrow. Day warm and pleasant.

Tuesday, September 30. At 8 O'clock this morning we was on the road towards Fort Scott. Our wagons was loaded with corn. I was detailed to act in the capacity of Sergeant Major on this expedition. At sun set we camped, fifteen miles from the Fort. . . .

Wednesday, October 1. This morning early we was all on the move at 4 O'clock this evening we arrived at the Fort and camp. We found the boys here who were captured, they was kept prisoners one night and day, then they was paroled but their horses were retained by Mayfield. They said they was well treated. Day quite warm.

Beginning October 2, Porter and his company accompanied General Blunt south into northern Arkansas and did not return to their Fort Scott station till April, 1863. Only essential diary entries from this period are included here.

Thursday, October 2. Today we had orders to pack up and be ready to move without delay. There is a large force now camped here and indications point to a forward move. At 5 O'clock P.M. the entire command was on the move in a southerly direction at dark we camped. Our company escorted our train out. Day quite warm.

Friday, October 3. This morning early the entire command was on the march. We kept on the move until 11 O'clock in the night arriving at Lamar, here we camped, and soon cooking and coffee making was the order of business. Our march today was over some fine country. The day hot and windy.

Saturday, October 4. This morning early we arose from our slumber wet and cold from exposure to a heavy rain during the night. At 10 O'clock A.M. we was on the road to Carthage. The troops was in command of Gen. Jas. G. Blunt. Train moved slow today, causing the troops to do likewise. At 11 O'clock tonight we camped near Spring river. The day cold and cloudy.

Sunday, October 5. Frosty this morning. On arising from my slumbers I found an unwelcome companion in my blanket by my side after a careful survey of his proportions I found him to be an eighteen year old Rattlesnake. I soon dissolved companionship with him by giving him sole possession of my bed. As soon as I gained my feet I set to work of doing some killing with out any orders from a Major General. I soon dispatched his snakeship and then eat breakfast. At 12 O'clock the order was to move forward. At 1 O'clock we crossed Spring River and passed through Carthage at 3 O'clock P.M. Our commander had suspicions that the enemy was laying on a woods nearby, ordered some artillery to shell the woods as no enemy appeared we continued on our way. At 5 O'clock P.M. we took a south course towards Newtonia[1] at 6 O'clock P.M. we camped near a creek. Day warm.

1. In east central Newton County, Mo.

Monday, October 6. This morning at 8 O'clock our Regiment left the command and took the advance as escort to the Pay Master. We left the train consisting of 300 wagons in command of Col. Cloud 2nd Kansas Cav. at 2½ O'clock P.M. we passed through Granby[1] a town situated in a lead mining district in Newton Co., Mo. The place was deserted and building dilapidated. At 4 O'clock P.M. we arrived at Newtonia in Newton Co. We then took a westerly course ten miles and joined the main command at 9 O'clock P.M. when camped. Our journey was through hilly and timber country. Day hot.

1. The Missouri State Guard obtained lead directly from the Granby mines in the first year of the war.

Tuesday, October 7. This morning we put up our tents for the first time since leaving Fort Scott. I know not how long we are to remain here. Our camp is on Indian Creek.[1] There was nothing more to note of the doings of today. The day was pleasant.

1. Indian Creek flows southwestward through southern Newton and McDonald counties, entering Elk River and eventually Grand River in Oklahoma.

Wednesday, October 8. This morning there was a heavy rainfall. At 10 O'clock A.M. our Company was paid by Major Eaton U.S.A. Soon after four Regiments of Cherokee Indians joined our forces. A cold rain fall continued throughout the day. There was a false alarm this evening causing some commotion with the troops. *(The uneventful next eight days are omitted.)*

Friday, October 17. This morning early we had marching orders to be ready to move at 7 O'clock A.M. Preparations were immediately made for our departure, at 7 O'clock we was on the march. After a march of 8 miles we arrived at Keetsville[1] in Barry Co., Mo. At 11 O'clock A.M. We halted and cooked twenty-four hours rations. At 10 O'clock tonight we was ordered forward. Our Regiment took the advance. . . .

1. In western Barry County, Mo., destroyed in the war; rebuilt in 1868 and renamed Washburn.

Saturday, October 18. After marching all night we arrived at Pea Ridge[1] at 6½ O'clock this morning, this being the place where the great battle was fought. We halted here and had breakfast. At 8 O'clock A.M. we moved forward a mile and camped. Today pleasant. *(The uneventful next nine days omitted.)*

1. In northern Benton County, Ark., site of the decisive Union victory March 7-8, 1862.

Tuesday, October 28. This morning early our Regiment and Brigade to which we was attached was in readiness for a forward move. At 9 O'clock A.M. our entire Brigade was marching on, at 5 O'clock P.M. we camped at Bentonville[1] Arkansas making 15 miles today. Today pleasant. *(The 29th is omitted.)*

1. Seat of Benton County, Ark.

Thursday, October 30. Our Brigade was again on the move at 8 O'clock this morning. We had a refreshing sleep out on the ground last night. After a tedious march we arrived at Maysville[1] at 9 O'clock P.M. This place was much dilapidated. It is situated on the line of the Indian Territory and Arkansas. We joined Blue Brigade and camped in the Indian Territory. Today pleasant.

1. In northwestern Benton County, Ark.

Friday, October 31. This morning at 5 O'clock

our Brigade and Blunts started on the road towards Pea Ridge. Why we take the back track I know not. We camped 8 miles from Bentonville. Our advance was attacked by the enemy, the boys stood by them and made short work with them, killing one of their men and took one prisoner. The day pleasant. *(Nov. 1-5 are omitted.)*

Thursday, November 6. This morning at 4½ O'clock George Priest[1] a member of my company died at the Hospital. He was a good and faithful member of the company and we feel sorry to loose [sic] his companionship. The company that remained in camp gave him a decent burial in a wood nearby. There was nothing farther transpired with us. I am no better. Day pleasant. *(Nov. 7-12 are omitted.)*

1. Private George Priest, Reedsburg, Wis., died at "Camp Bowen, Ark." of disease.

Thursday, November 13. This morning at 7 O'clock our Brigade was again on the move. After marching 20 miles in a south course we camped at 4 O'clock P.M. on the edge of a beautiful prairie near a good stream of water at about dark my company with others started for Cane Hill[1] 30 miles distant to reconnoiter. I accompanied them, but did not feel well. Today pleasant.

1. Now Canehill, a community in southwest Washington County, Ark.

Friday, November 14. After a lively march last night we came upon the enemies picket a short distance from Cane Hill, we captured one of the picket and the others escaped. We then quickened our pace to a gallop. Our entering Cane Hill and passing a brick building or Seminary a heavy volley of musketry was fired upon us by about 300 of the enemy in the building, we returned the fire when passing. Only one of our number was wounded slightly. We soon discovered 7000 more of the enemy camped near by and rallying to arms, soon sending some shot and shell over us without effect we soon escaped in the darkness and started for camp to report our discovery. Arrived at camp this evening. . . . *(Nov. 15-19 are omitted.)*

Thursday, November 20. Last night a heavy frost came but today pleasant and sunshine. Our Company went out foraging today. I did not accompany them as I did not feel well enough. I wrote a letter to my sister Cornelia today. All quiet in camp.

Friday, November 21. This forenoon I was idle. Afternoon I wrote a letter to my cousin Antoinette King.[1] The day was clear and pleasant. Some frost last night. I felt some better today. *(Nov. 22-25 omitted.)*

1. Resident of Batavia, Wis.

Wednesday, November 26. This morning an ambulance came in with two men of Co. "D" of our Regt who was wounded last night. They report that at

8 O'clock last night our scouts encountered 400 or more of the enemy when a brisk engagement took place. The enemy was soon put to flight their loss not known; ours resulted as above stated in two wounded, Geo. R. Kelley.[1] Geo. W. Kelly[2] and John Finnigan[3] who had been reported as deserters arrived in camp this afternoon and A. Russell[4] a new recruit. A supply train came also. Day cool.

1. Private George R. Kelley, Baraboo, Wis.
2. Private George W. Kelley, Winfield, Wis.
3. Private John Finnigan, Baraboo, Wis.
4. Private Andrew M. Russell, Baraboo, Wis.

Thursday, November 27. Our ears was greeted with the welcome and long looked for orders to prepare for a forward move at an early hour this morning. We soon struck our tents and partook of our breakfast, when all the Brigades was on the move our destination was Cane Hill as the enemy was reported in heavy force. Our train corralled after moving a mile. At 9 O'clock our company and others was left in charge of the train and the main force continued on. Day cool. *(Nov. 28 is omitted.)*

Saturday, November 29. We learn that our forces met the enemy yesterday at Cane Hill and a fearful engagement took place which resulted in the utter defeat and route [sic] of the enemy, our forces pursued and captured many of them as prisoners. Lieut Col. Jewell of a Kansas Regt. fell mortally wounded. I did not learn the amount of killed and wounded on either side. At 8 O'clock this morning we was ordered to move forward and join our main command, at 9 O'clock A.M. we was on the road, at 11 O'clock A.M. we crossed the Illinois River,[1] Ark. At 1 O'clock P.M. we made a short halt at a small town called Cincinnati,[2] Ark. After a fatiguing journey we arrived at the main command at Rhaes Mills,[3] Ark. . . . *(Nov. 30 is omitted.)*

1. The Illinois flows westward from Benton and Washington counties, Ark., entering Grand River in Oklahoma.
2. A community in northwest Washington County, Ark.
3. Modern Rhea, in western Washington County, Ark.

Monday, December 1. This morning 16 of our Company and Lieut. [Clark] Willsey[1] went with others to Huntsville, Ark.[2] and Fayetteville[3] under orders. The day was quite cold. I went to Brooks tent this afternoon when Mrs. Brooks set before me some Pancakes and honey a treat seldom met with to surprise the stomach of a soldier. Our Brigade was ordered to wear the usual badge of mourning for Lieut. Col. Jewell of our Brigade who died of wounds received at Cane Hill. *(Dec. 2-6 are omitted.)*

1. Clark B. Wilsey, Baraboo, Wis., sergeant, afterwards first lieutenant.
2. Seat of Madison County, Ark.
3. Seat of Washington County, Ark.

Sunday, December 7. This morning at 3 O'clock five companies of us was in our saddles and on the road to Cane Hill once more. At daylight we arrived there and the sun had not risen when our whole command joined us and we was immediately placed in battle array. We waited anxiously for the enemy to appear. Soon cannonading was heard east of us. We was then ordered by General Blunt to fall back to Rhaes Mill to save our train from capture. On our arrival we found all safe. I was ordered immediately to take a portion of my Company and take the advance toward Fayetteville. I had not gone far when I came upon the left of the Confederate line of battle fully engaged in battle with General [Francis] Herrons[1] force of 7000 men. The enemy numbered 35000 under command of Genls. [Thomas] Hindman[2] and [John S.] Marmaduke[3]. I sent word back to Genl. Blunt who hurried up his force and we was soon engaged in a terrific strife. Herrons exhausted troops gave us a hearty cheers for coming to their assistance and fought with reserved [sic] vigor. The hills and valley now shook with the shock of battle and heavy cannonading. Our force was now 12000. The scene was grand and indescribable. Night closed the scene of strife. I captured two of the enemy after dark. Our loss was 700 killed and 2000 wounded. The enemy lost 1500 killed and 3000 wounded. The enemy retreated from the field as soon as dark set in. We spent the night caring for our wounded. This was necessarily sad work to perform and the night cold and frosty. . . .

1. Major General Francis Jay Herron commanded two Federal divisions during this, the Battle of Prairie Grove.

2. Major General Thomas C. Hindman commanded the Confederate Trans-Mississippi Department.
3. Major General John Sappington Marmaduke, CSA.

Monday, December 8. This morning before day I started with my Company and two prisoners to Hd Quarters of Genl Blunt and turned my prisoners over to the care of the General. We then got some breakfast and fed our horses, after which we was sent out to reconnoiter the enemies position. We found a portion of the enemy on the Van Buren[1] road, we suppose they are the rear of the retreating foe. We found many of the enemies dead and wounded on the road. At noon we reported results to Genl. Blunt. Afternoon the enemy had retired leaving their dead unburied. A burying party was busy a burying our dead today. We camped near the battlefield. This battle is called Prairie Grove, Ark.[2] Today pleasant.

1. Seat of Crawford County, Ark.
2. A community 11 miles southwest of Fayetteville, Ark.

Tuesday, December 9. This morning early we went over the battlefield and found many of the enemy dead scattered about and in some places thickly strewn where the conflict raged fiercest. A ghastly spectacle it was, as every degree of mutilated bodies presented themselves. I repaired to a large building nearby where the enemy had located their Hospital. I found the building full of wounded and many outside begging piteously for the Surgeons attention. The Surgeons were busy amputating and binding up wounds. And the hogs were devouring the limbs that were thrown out of the Hospital in a heap for burial. I now surveyed the horrible scene around me and realized the horrors of war in all its aspects. Afternoon we returned to Rhaes Mill our former camp. Blunts command all joined us about dark, our company is now attached to Blunts Command. Day pleasant.

Wednesday, December 10. Last night I went with my Company and Co.'s "L" and "E" of our Regt. to Cane Hill to reconnoiter for the enemy. We found none there, returned this morning and reported results. We learn today that Genl. [Alexander] Steen[1] and Major Chen[2] of the enemy were killed in the late battle. The battle ground was in part on Tilleys prairie south of Fayetteville, 8 miles. The 20th Wis. Infantry, the 26th Indiana, 36 & 92 Ill. and 19th Iowa Infantry, 10th & 13th Kansas and 10th Ill. Cavalry was terribly cut up or lost heavily at the late battle. All quiet in camp. Today pleasant. *(Dec. 11-20 are omitted.)*

1. Brigadier General Alexander Early Steen, formerly lieutenant colonel in the Missouri State Guard.
2. Unidentified.

Sunday, December 21. Today I was employed making a coffin for John G. Hutchins[1] who died at our Regimental Hospital last evening. He was one of our last recruits from Wis. We buried him in the cemetery at Cane Hill with military honors at sunset. Lieut Clark

B. Willsey went to Rhaes Mill and returned this evening. Today was pleasant. *(Dec. 22-26 are omitted.)*

1. John C. Hutchins, Woodland, Wis., died Dec. 20 at Cane Hill, Ark., of disease.

Saturday, December 27. This morning early the entire command was prepared to move out. At 8 O'clock A.M. we started in a southerly direction. At 10 O'clock A.M. we was marching over a portion of the Boston Mountain[1] on the road to Van Buren. This afternoon our course lay through a valley between the mountains. A stream called Cove Creek took a meandering course through this valley which we crossed 20 times today. After marching 20 miles we camped at 9 O'clock P.M. Today quite pleasant.

1. The Boston Mountains, a prominent range of the Ozarks Mountains between Fayetteville and Van Buren.

Sunday, December 28. The reveille called us from our slumbers at 3 O'clock this morning. We soon had breakfast, fed and saddle our horses, and at 5 O'clock A.M. by Genl Blunts orders our Company took the advance of the moving mass of humanity. We crossed Cove Creek 7 times before daylight. At sunrise we crossed the Crow River a beautiful stream. After crossing we halted and built fires of rails to warm as there was a heavy frost this morning and ground frozen. The 9th Wisconsin Infantry soon came up and forded the river when we gave them our fire today by and warm [sic] at 7 O'clock we started again passing Genl. Herrins command, when we was ordered to double quick, we soon came upon the enemies picket, 3 in number ten miles from Van Buren. We captured them and pushed on at a lively speed, our Cavalry being in command of Col. Cloud. We came upon a Regiment of the enemy in camp 8 miles from Van Buren, we charged upon the camp and killed many while many made their escape. We captured many and was soon in possession of their camp, horses, Quarter Master and Commissary Stores, Guns, Ammunition, Wagons and Ambulances. They left their breakfast cooking. We soon started in pursuit of the retreating foe and found wagons and other vehicles upset and otherwise left on the road so that nothing should hinder their escape. Our Regiment and other [sic] arrived at Van Buren at 2 O'clock P.M. Col. Cloud took a portion of Cavalry and pursued the enemy through town capturing some prisoners. We found the enemy in force under Genl. Hindsman on the opposite side of the river, or I should say Arkansas River. All quiet in town when we arrived. At a quarter to 4 O'clock P.M. the enemy brought a battery to bare [sic] on the town and commenced shelling the place without warning the citizens. The result was one soldier of the 2nd Kansas Cav. and a young lady was killed, besides driving the inmates of their Hospital to a place of safety. Our Batteries soon got in position and rained shot and shell into the enemies camp, and in a half hour the enemies battery was silent. Our Batteries continued to shell the enemies position compelling him to fall back to some more congenial spot. At sunset the firing eased. At 10 O'clock this evening a heavy cannonading took place a short distance below us. I suppose to keep the opposite shore to [sic] hot for the enemy to locate in. The boys found a building containing a large quantity of liquors, soon a great many was drunk before a stop was put to it by a guard. We camped in town. Today pleasant.

Monday, December 29. We passed through the night without any disturbance from the enemy. The cannonading we heard last evening was for the purpose of dislodging a small camp of the enemy opposite the town. The enemy soon found themselves in a uncomfortable position and moved away at a lively pace. This morning two steamboats laden with Quarter Master Commissary and other stores came up the river for supplying the enemy. They not being aware of our occupying the town came in range of our guns when a shot was fired across their bows, they made for the opposite side of the river and ran on a sand bar and the troops that was aboard jumped overboard to escape, our boys soon took possession of the boats and landed them at Van Buren. The names of the Steam Boats captured and burned at Van Buren, Ark. were as follows. Violet, Rose Douglas, Frederic Notreba, Erie No. 6 and Van Buren, five in number. During the day we captured two more steamers loaded with stores for the enemy. At dark Genl. Blunt ordered the boats to be burnt. Soon four large steamers and one steam ferry boat was wrapped in flames which presented a grand scene at about 8 O'clock. There was a large brick storehouse near, which took fire and was consumed and with it 150 lbs of Molasses and the town came near burning. The troops worked manfully and saved the place. We had orders to be ready to move at dark but our duties detained us. So when the fire had ceased we was ordered to camp until morning. Today pleasant.

Tuesday, December 30. This morning at 9½ O'clock we was again on the march back to Rhaes Mills. The day was so cold that we was compelled to wear our overcoats. Cloudy this morning and indications of snow. A large number of refugees and Negroes came with us from Van Buren, and they presented a terrible state of poverty and wretchedness. We returned by the same route we came, and the road was over hilly and rocky country today. We marched 25 miles today and camped at sunset, tired and hungry.

Wednesday, December 31. At daylight we was again on the road. We had a cold and uncomfortable night and but little sleep as we had no tents with us. The ground was frozen enough to bear a horse and rider. Our march today was by the Boston Mountains and across the same streams we met with on our march to Van Buren. We did not see the sun until 10 O'clock A.M. on account of the mountain height. These mountains are in many respects sublime in appearance. They are quite rocky, some of the rocks have a perpendicular height of 100 feet or more, while many are shelving and ragged covered with pine and cedar besides other kinds of trees. Fred A. Copeland[1] of our

Company lost his horse and was obliged to appropriate a donkey for his use. The only way he could keep the lazy beast up with the Company was to put an ear of corn on the end of a cane stalk and hold it in front of the animal, when he would hasten to overtake it. The boys gave Fred the name of "Balaam," a name he did not fancy, and in order to get rid of the accursed name he disposed of the beast on arriving at Camp. After a march of 30 miles today we arrived at our old camp ground at Rhaes Mills at a little before sunset.

1. Private Frederic A. Copeland, Baraboo, Wis.

❦ 1863 ❦

Thursday, January 1. A new year has dawned upon us, and with it war still in progress. I set about to enjoy the day as my limited means would admit. I took a few drinks of brandy to stimulate my exertions, I procured some canned peaches and oysters at the Sutlers and soon surprised the vacancies of the inner man. During the day I received my Commission as 2nd Lieutenant of Co. "L" 3rd Regt. Wis. Cavalry and the consequence was I was elected to do some treating. Many of the boys in and about our Regiment partook freely of "Coffin Varnish" and many rows occurred during the day. I was with my companions until a late hour and a jolly carouse we had. The day was cloudy windy and some sleet. At dark we had marching orders for the morrow.

Friday, January 2. It rained nearly all night. Early this morning the reveille called us forth to our morning duties and prepare for another move. Our Company was detailed to take charge of a herd of Government Cattle and proceeded to Fayetteville, the county seat of Washington County, Ark. At 10 O'clock A.M. we started, and passed over some nice country and saw some good farms. After marchng 18 miles we arrived at Fayetteville at 8 O'clock P.M. The place has the appearance of once being in a flourishing and quite a prosperous condition. But war had done its work of devastation in the business portion, as the Confederate Genl. McColloch[1] had burnt it. Orderly Sergt. E. M. Cooper[2] and myself fortunately found a place of comfort for the night with a family. We had a good warm supper and a nice bed on the floor before the fire. Today pleasant.

1. Brigadier General Ben McCulloch, the former Texas Ranger, was killed in the Battle of Pea Ridge in March, 1862.

2. Eli M. Cooper, Baraboo, Wis., afterwards Second Lieutenant.

Saturday, January 3. I was up quite early this morning, after a good sound sleep. Our hostess provided us a good breakfast. At 10 O'clock A.M. we was ordered to take our stock to Elm Springs[1] and we immediately moved forward in a northerly course through some beautiful farming country and good timber. After marching 12 miles we arrived at Elm Springs Mill an hour before sunset and camped. This place has but few building and a large Flouring Mill. Our entire force camped here to night. Today pleasant. *(Jan. 4 through 6 are omitted.)*

1. In north central Washington County, Ark.

Wednesday, January 7. This forenoon our forces here was preparing for review in the afternoon when we passed in review by Genl. [John M.] Schofield[1] our Departmental Commander. Infantry Artillery and Cavalry in order marched in a continual line until sunset, where the last column passed the Generals notice. Tonight the officers had a grand dance and superb supper in honor of our General Schofield.

During the early part of the evening some drunken soldiers stoned the building where the dancing was. General Schofield was hit on the head disqualifying him somewhat from enjoying the entertainment. I learn that the perpetrators of this foul act were of a Kent. Regt. There was a number of others hit at the time but no one seriously hurt. I was ordered with my Company to guard the locality against farther assault. At supper I was provided with a plenty of green peas, hot biscuit and butter, cakes and pie. Well, I soon struck a business like attitude and these fine rations soon vanished from the dishes that was provided for their reception to a place long since deprived of these luxuries. Today very cool. I was on duty all night.

1. Brigadier (afterwards Major) General John M. Schofield, commanded the Army of the Frontier and District of Southwest Missouri.

Thursday, January 8. I took a little sleep this morning and got up for breakfast. My eyes continue very sore so I did not do much duty today. Orderly Cooper had cause to tie James G. Winters[1] of Company to a fence with his hands tied behind him, drunkenness and disorderly conduct was the cause. Today pleasant but cool. *(Jan. 9-22 are omitted.)*

1. Private James G. Winters, Baraboo, Wis., discharged for disability Mar. 4.

Friday, January 23. This morning at 5 O'clock

our Company and Companies "K" and "E" of our Regt. crossed the river War Eagle,[1] not quite swimming our horses. We was all across before daylight. We then learned that some Bushwhackers was at a house three miles away, so we went out to capture them, but did not find them, but took a man and his wife from the house, who was suspected of being allied to the clan. We returned to the river over hills and ravines, and turned our capture over to the Genl. Blunt. We found the command still crossing the river so we took the position of Rear Guard today. The road was in a fearful condition by so large a body of troops and the heavy train passing over it. The rear had the most trying ordeal to accomplish the passage. The road today was over hills and deep ravines. The hills are covered with a heavy growth of Pitch Pine trees. We camped an hour before sunset in a apple orchard about one mile from White river.[2] Our course was north today. This morning some stormy but the day was clear and warm. *(Jan. 24-Feb. 22 are omitted.)*

1. War Eagle Creek rises in southern Madison County, Ark., and flows generally northward into White River.

2. White River rises in northwest Arkansas, flows northeastward into southern Missouri, then southeastward back into Arkansas, entering the Mississippi.

Monday, February 23. This morning the wind was blowing hard and very cold, and the ground was froze. Immediately after we had breakfast we again moved forward as yesterday in a northwest course and crossed two prairies during the forenoon. At noon we crossed Honey Creek and at 3 O'clock P.M. we arrived at Mt. Vernon the county seat of Lawrence County, Mo. Stephen D. Jarvis[1] a member of my Company was taken sick on the march and we placed him in the Hospital at this place. The large brick Court House of Mt. Vernon was used for the purpose. We passed through this beautiful place and soon after camped. Today cloudy and cold. *(Feb. 23-Mar. 24 are omitted.)*

1. Private Stephen D. Jarvis, Excelsior, Wis., died at Mt. Vernon April 7.

Wednesday, March 25. This morning Lieut. Willsey took 24 men and joined 80 others of our Regiment and two Companies of the 9th Wis. Infantry and started on an expedition to Berryville[1] distant 15 miles to drive out 400 Rebels said to be there. This morning our team attempted to cross White River for forage and lost one mule. One teamster came near being drowned in crossing the river. . . .

1. Berryville, Ark., seat of Carroll County, some 50 miles south of Mt. Vernon.

Thursday, March 26. This morning the scouting party that went to Berryville returned, bringing one prisoner supposed to be a Captain of a Bush-whacking band. They report having run the enemy from Berryville. The troops was engaged ferrying forage over White River today. Some Companies of the 9th

Wis. started on an expedition last evening. One year ago our Regiment left the State of Wisconsin. Day pleasant. *(Mar. 27-29 are omitted.)*

Tuesday, March 31. Carrollton[1] the county seat of Carroll Co., Ark., is a dilapidated place. The Court House once a fine brick structure had been destroyed and war had stopped the business of the place. I took command of a foraging party and went 8 miles south of camp and secured abundance of corn, hams, chickens and horses. On our way out we was fired upon by Bushwhackers from a bluff by the roadside wounding one teamster in the leg and killed one mule. I pursued the devils and killed two, their Capt. Bobo[2] jumped down the bluff on rocks disfiguring his face and breaking his legs and one arm. I placed him in care of the wounded teamster to be taken in camp who said he would be damned well cared for, and I think he took care to give him a damned good shaking over the rough road. Today pleasant.

1. In southeast Carroll County, then the county seat.
2. Unidentified.

Wednesday, April 1. I turned my prisoner over to Genl. Blunt on my arrival at camp yesterday, and found all the Cavalry and a detachment with two Howitzers had been sent to Crooked Creek in search of a large camp of Bushwhackers said to be in that locality. A Dispatch came in this morning stating that our Cavalry and Howitzer boys came upon a camp of the enemy of about 500 men 24 miles from camp at 12 O'clock last night, and opened on them with shot and shell and charged them when the enemy endeavored to escape. Our men captured a large number of prisoners, horses, saddles, guns, blankets and clothing, besides their camp equipage, teams and wagons. They pursued the enemy 3 miles and on account of the dark abandoned farther pursuit. This morning I sent Qr. Mr. Sergt. S. Wheeler[1] with 10 men, Orderly Cooper 10, and Sergt. Stansfield[2] with 10 men on a scout. Our forage party was fired into today, no one hurt. Another party of the 9th Wis. was fired into by guerrillas and one of the boys was mortally wounded. Today terribly windy. *(Apr. 2-3 are omitted.)*

1. Stephen Wheeler, Baraboo, Wis., quartermaster sergeant.
2. William Stansfield, Ironton, Wis., quartermaster sergeant.

Saturday, April 4. Last night as our Scouts was returning to camp one of our pickets mistook them for the enemy and fired a shot at them but luckily without harm. Our camp was aroused to arms, but on learning the cause of alarm we was dismissed. This morning there was some frost. We was ordered to march at 7½ O'clock A.M. Capt. Thomas Derry[1] of Co. "L" commanding the expedition. At the time appointed we started on our way, in a south course. Some after starting Col. Wm. Wier[2] in temporary command of our Brigade sent us a Dispatch ordering our transportation back and we continue our march to Clear Creek.[3] At noon we stopped to feed our horses and wait the arrival of Capt. [Leander] Shaw[4] and his Co. "D" who had been scouting since morning, they came to us at 5 O'clock P.M. and we resumed our march. I was in command of the advance guard and at sunset I came upon twelve of the enemy who fired upon us without doing injury, we returned the fire killing two and wounding one and capturing him and two more, the balance escaped in the brush. The prisoners claim to belong to Genl. Marmaduke command. We took 5 more prisoners about dark. At 10 O'clock P.M. we camped having marched 16 miles. Today warm.

1. Captain Thomas Derry, Middleton, Wis., commanding Company L.

2. Colonel William Weer, 4th Kansas Regiment (mixed infantry, cavalry, mounted infantry, and some artillery).

3. Obviously not the familiar Vernon County Clear Creek. There are Clear Creeks in Greene and Lawrence counties.

4. Captain Leander J. Shaw, Mukwango, Wis., commanding Company D, settled in Vernon County after the war and held public office.

Sunday, April 5. Early this morning a trial was had with the prisoners and 3 of the number proved to be guerrillas and were sentenced to be shot. There was a detail of two men from each of our Companies to execute the sentence. I was ordered to take charge of the execution of these Knights of the brush. As soon as the command started I marched the three Prisoners out by the road side and formed my men in convenient position to perform the duty assigned us. I read the proceedings and sentence of the trial and the doomed men made no reply, but started to run when the boys fired upon them with their carbine killing them instantly. We then joined the command and after one short march we halted for breakfast. I took breakfast at a citizens. I was ordered to take charge of the Advance Guard and soon after starting I came upon a fellow in the road. The man was cleanly and well dressed in a new and gray uniform of the Confederate Army. On questioning and examining his papers I found he was a Confederate Soldier on furlough. I turned over to our Commander who paroled him.[1] In the afternoon we arrived within 6 miles of Yellville the County Seat of Marion Co., Ark., here we halted a short time supposing we was near the enemies picket. I was ordered to take a circuitous route with 12 men and cut off the escape of the picket, but we failed to find the picket or camp of the enemy so we continued onto town. At 4 O'clock P.M. we surprised the towns people by charging in sudden upon them. No troops or enemy was found here. I came upon a Confederate Lieut. at a hotel of the place. He was on leave of absence from his Company and had consumption. We took him prisoner. We compelled the citizens to furnish us with supper, and at sunset we left the place. This place is very beautiful having many fine buildings. The Court House, a brick structure and some buildings had been burnt. We camped at 10 O'clock P.M. Marched 24 miles.

1. This grotesquely inconsistent policy was typical of

defiance by Federal field officers of official Lincoln government policy, based on the advice of experts in military law, making minimal distinction between guerrillas and regulars.

Monday, April 6. This morning at 5 O'clock we again moved forward. At noon we halted and eat dinner and breakfast together, after which my Company and Co "D" was ordered to scout through the country. We soon captured three men and horses whom we found secreted in the woods. I sent my Company forward while I took Bro. Walworth, A. D. Kimbal,[1] C. H. Davis[2] and Wm Wood[3] with me and took a different route. I soon came upon two negroes and 9 horses in the timber and took them with us, besides the owner of the captured property whom we found near by in the brush. His name was Young, and a guerrilla Capt. We found a cave in a bluff containing clothing and bedding, belonging to Young and we took such as we required for our use and joined our Company and soon joined our Command. We found a Powder Mill where the enemy manufactured powder and burnt it and another building attached to it. We camped at 10 O'clock P.M. I am unable to tell the distance gone over today.

1. Private Augustus D. Kimball, Baraboo, Wis.
2. Private Charles H. Davis, Baraboo, Wis.
3. Private William P. R. Wood, Woodland, Wis.

Tuesday, April 7. This morning the officers was ordered to assemble in Courtmartial to try our prisoners. Four took the oath of allegiance and was released, and we decided to take the Lieut and six others to Head Quarters. At 11 O'clock A.M. we again moved forward. I was placed in Command of the prisoners guard. We marched 10 miles and camped before sunset. The days are warm, nights cold, roads dusty, country hilly and timbered and some nice farms on our road.

Wednesday, April 8. Last evening two parties came in camp who had been sent out in search of us. They soon returned to Carrollton. This morning after breakfast we started for Carrollton 13 miles distant. The day was rainy, arrived at the Command at noon. We found our Captain D. S. Vittum[1] in camp just arrived from Leavenworth and Wm H. Gardner[2] from furlough and A. Letcher[3] and two recruits for Co. Afternoon a horse race was again indulged in by the boys. We made our quarters in houses. I enjoyed a visit with the Captain.

1. David S. Vittum, Baraboo, Wis., Captain of Co. F.
2. Private William H. Gardner, Baraboo, Wis.
3. Private Joseph H. Letcher, Baraboo, Wis.

Friday, April 10. This morning at 7½ O'clock our command was again on the move. After marching two miles our advance guard came upon a party of Bushwhackers and killed one and took two prisoners. We arrived at Dubuque[1] at 10 O'clock A.M. This place is a steam boat landing on White River in Ark. but too small to carry the name, five or six poor dilapidated buildings made up its gigantic proportions. We continued our journey and an hour before sunset we arrived at Forsythe and camped. This place is the County Seat of Taney Co., Mo. and situated on White River, but a small place. Today pleasant.

1. Near the mouth of West Sugar Loaf Creek, east of Yellville, Ark.

Saturday, April 11. This morning before day it commenced to rain very heavy, but cleared off by sunrise. I was not busy this forenoon. Afternoon I walked out to view the place and surrounding. I found the town in a decayed condition. It is located on a flat by the river, and Swan Creek runs from north around west and empties in White river which passes the south side of town; while a range of high bluffs and hills pass around from east to north and west of the place, those to the west are 200 feet high. The troops that are camped here are the 19th Iowa Infantry 9th Wis. Infantry, two Companies of 1st Iowa Cavalry, Co's. "A", "D", "E", "F", "K" and "L" of 3rd Wis. Cav. and two Howitzer detachments of our Regt. all in comand of old Billy Wier of 10th Kansas Infantry. Our Regt was on parade at 5 O'clock P.M. Today pleasant. *(Apr. 12-14 are omitted.)*

Wednesday, April 15. Today I was pasting up my Co. accounts. The majority of our Cavalry was out scouting and foraging. Wm Gardner a member of my Company had an attack of delirious tremors this evening. He had been on a prolonged drunk of late and being an accomplished jig and Clog dancer he was

furnished whiskey for an exhibition of these feats. . . .
(Apr. 16 and 17 are omitted.)

Saturday, April 18. At 9 O'clock last evening I was relieved from picket by a new guard. I remained at the Mill until this morning when I returned to camp. On my arrival I learned that two of Capt. Offs. Co. "K" had been found killed and laying in the road about 14 miles from camp. More informal work of guerrillas but we get in some good work with them to make up for our loss. I spent the afternoon making up my Co. Returns. Today cool and some rain this afternoon. *(Apr. 19-21 are omitted.)*

Wednesday, April 22. Our infantry started out for Springfield[1] this morning. Soon after I went in Company with Capt. Shaw towards Carrollton, Ark. Our road was mostly over mountain country interspersed with pine trees. No farms visible until near night, when we came up with the command and camped 9 miles from Carrollton. I procured a good supper at a farmers. Marched 31 miles today. Some troops was sent to burn Carrollton tonight which they done effectually. Today quite hot.

1. Seat of Greene County, Mo. the region's leading community.

Thursday, April 23. We was ordered to march to Hartsville[1] at 7 A.M. when our Comd started on the back track and at night passed through Forsythe, Mo.

and camped. Both men and horses are short of rations and forage and great complaint is heard among the men and curses are heaped upon the Commissary and Quarter Master. . . . *(Apr. 24-25 are omitted.)*

1. Hartville, seat of Wright County, Mo.

Sunday, April 26. At 12 O'clock last night a Militia Lieutenant and 30 men came in our camp unobserved by our picket, and some little excitement was rife among the men until satisfied who they were. They remained with us until morning. At 7 O'clock A.M. our command again moved forward. We had some difficulty in crossing the Gasconade[1] as the water was deep and swift current. We swam our horses. One ambulance nearly swamped, loosing one wheel broke. Our negro Joe[2] came up with old Lize his mule, loaded with chickens and corn fodder and soon Joe and mule disappeared beneath the turbid waters, but soon came up and made the landing amid the cheers and gibs [sic] of the boys, but the chickens were drowned. After a march of 12 miles and crossing the river 5 times we reached Hartsville, Mo. at noon. Saw many improved farms today. Rainy last night and this morning. I camped in a vacant building.

1. The Gasconade rises in Webster County, Mo., flowing northeastward into the Missouri River in Gasconade County.

2. Unidentified.

Monday, April 27. Not being engaged in my

duty today, so I took a walk about the town of Hartsville the county seat of Wright Co., Mo. The place I found nearly deserted by its inhabitance. The buildings were in a tolerable good condition though many had been injured by shot and shell during an engagement last winter with Marmadukes force of 3000 against 200 Federals, resulting in a victory for the latter, and retreat of the former. I found on examination that the large brick Court House had been pierced by 10 cannon shot and shells. The town had the appearance of being a business place before the late unpleasantness.

Tuesday, April 28. Last evening at sunset, I was ordered with 10 men to bear a dispatch from Col. Wier our Brigade commander to Genl. Herron at Salem, Mo. We started on our dark and dangerous expedition immediately and with the many dangers on our way we crossed the Gasconade Whetstone and Beaver by swimming our horses but without accident. We continued our journey until this morning at 8 O'clock when we arrived at Dannins Mill, on Big Piney Creek,[1] here we stopped two hours for rest and to feed our horses. After which I learned by some troops I met here that there was no danger ahead, so I sent C. B. Foster[2] of my Co. and another man to Salem,[3] 30 miles from Houston.[4] I continued my trip 3 miles and arrived at Houston and stopped for comd. to arrive. Camped in a vacant house and dined with a citizen. . . .

1. Big Piney River rises in southern Texas County, Mo., and flows north into the Gasconade.

2. Private Charles S. Foster, Baraboo, Wis.
3. Seat of Dent County, Mo.
4. Seat of Texas County, Mo.

Wednesday, April 29. I took a stroll about town this morning and found but two families living here. A few troops made the sole population. Houston, the county seat of Texas County, Mo. and located on a branch of Big Piney which runs through a portion of the town, is beautifully situated, has a large brick Court House and other fine buildings. Our Co. arrived with our Brigade this forenoon and camped. I found my Capt. D. S. Vittum quite unwell. Lieut. Willsey had gone home to Wis. on leave. . . . *(Apr. 30 omitted.)*

Friday, May 1. At 6 O'clock this morning our command was again on the move. We crossed Current River[1] three times and entered a deep ravine with high bluffs on either side for a distance of 15 miles on our route after which we came upon table land. Arrived at Salem the County Seat of Dent Co., Mo. at 2 P.M. and camped. . . . *(May 2-5 are omitted.)*

1. Current River rises in Texas County and flows southeastward into White River in Arkansas.

Wednesday, May 6. This morning A. C. Kent[1] a Q.M. of our Regiment and myself started at 9 O'clock for Rolla to be mustered in, myself as 2nd Lieut. About 13 miles from Salem we passed the camp of the 20th Wis. Infantry and other Regts. about noon. At 4½

O'clock P.M. we arrived at Rolla the County Seat of Phelps Co., Mo. and present terminus of the St. Louis, Rolla and Springfield Rail Road. We learn that this place is 25 miles from Salem. Genl. Herron had his troops and Head Quarters here.

1. Arthur C. Kent, Janesville, Wis., battalion quartermaster sergeant.

Thursday, May 7. This morning Lieut. Kent and myself went to the Muster Office and was informed that we could not be mustered on account of a press of business and our case could not be attended to for some days. We then spent the day in Rolla and saw a train of cars arrive from St. Louis they being the first I had seen since the 6th of May, 1862. I now felt that I had once more arrived in a land of civilization. We received cheering news from Genl. Hooker on the Potomac. Saw many drunken soldiers today. . . . *(May 8 is omitted.)*

Saturday, May 9. This morning the news from Genl. Hooker are gloomy as he was forced back across the Rapahanoc.[1] Yet we are confident of a final victory over the enemy for the yanks are stubborn and will see to it that we accomplish our work. Our camp is quiet and day hot. *(May 10-13 are omitted.)*

1. A reference to the Confederate victory at Chancellorsville, May 1-4.

Thursday, May 14. At 9½ O'clock this

morning we started on our way. We kept down Current River and was obliged to cross it 21 times during the day, arrived at Eminence the County Seat of Shannon Co., Mo. at sunset. The Court House was a log structure and two stories high and the lone occupant of a woods. We passed on two miles and camped at Coxes farm. *(May 15-21 are omitted.)*

Friday, May 22. The escort with Gov. Solomon, Adjt. Genl Gaylord and Genl Herron & Brig Genl. Ewing came in camp this morning. This forenoon the companies and Regts. here are preparing for Review. At one O'clock P.M. 6 Companies of the 3rd Wis. Cav. the 19th Iowa Infantry the 9th Wis. Infantry Regt. and the 25th Ohio Battery and two Howitzer Detachments were Reviewed by Maj. Genl. Herron. Gov. Solomon, Adjt. Genl Gaylord and Brig. Genl Ewing[1] were present with Genl. Herron. After Review, the officers and Governor join in a social gathering and had an Army Love Feast by drinking Champagne. Today cloudy, afternoon rainy.

1. Brigadier General Thomas C. Ewing commanded the District of the Border headquartered in Kansas City.

Saturday, May 23. Today five new recruits joined our Company, came from Wisconsin. One of them Oscar Allen[1] of Baraboo, Wis. was an old Messmate of mine in the 1st Wisconsin Infantry Regt. I was glad to meet my old comrade again. We soon sat down to talk over our former experience and had a good time. Nothing more of interest today, but hot. *(May 24-June 6 are omitted.)*

1. Corporal Oscar Allen, according to the Roster a resident of Janesville, Wis.

Sunday, June 7. There was a heavy rain all day. I took a good sleep this afternoon. All quiet with us, and as far as we learn elsewhere in this State, with the exception of some bushwhacking parties who constantly maraud the State in search of plunder, besides committing murder and other crime, not countenanced by any of the civilized nations of Earth.

Monday, June 8. Transportation having arrived our Company struck tents and packed our equipage for a move to Rolla. Not having the necessary transportation to move the commissary stores, Capt. Vittum and Lieut. Willsey remained with the majority of the Company to guard them until they could be moved. I was sent with 8 men to guard the train to Rolla. At 10 O'clock I started with the Train, we moved out 8 miles on the road to Dry Fork Creek, and as it did not bear any resemblance to its name, it being full and out of its banks we was necessarily compelled to camp. Rainy all day. *(June 9-12 are omitted.)*

Saturday, June 13. As I was not otherwise engaged, I spent the greater portion of the day reading a Novel the title of which was the Unionist Daughter, and I found it interesting. . . .

Sunday, June 14. As I did not finish reading my Novel yesterday, I continued to peruse its pages today, not finding any other employment. Wm Gardners Wife came to our Company this morning from Wisconsin. She says that she is willing to undergo the hardships of a soldier that she may be with her husband. Many of our boys employed their time reading and card playing today. The day very hot.

Monday, June 15. This morning our Regiment had orders to move our camp three miles farther north where we could be provided with a good spring of water. The order was obeyed promptly. Our Camp is now on the east limits of Rolla. This afternoon I was engaged reading another Novel the title was Pauline of the Potomac or the McClellan Spy. Today was excessively hot.

Tuesday, June 16. This morning my Capt. had a difficulty with Major Schraeling[1] who was temporarily in command of Regiment. The quarrel originated out of the Major requiring to [sic] many unnecessary demands of the Officers which became obnoxious and we had determined to stop it. There was no farther excitement today. . . .

1. Major John C. Schroeling, Port Washington, Wis., commanding the third battalion of the Regiment.

Wednesday, June 17. This morning I formed the acquaintance of Miss Murdock a daughter of our

Sutler and lately from Janesville, Wis. on a visit to her father. I found the young lady amiable and fascinating. Well, I can not explain whither her beauty, or fascinating manners, made a very decided impression on me, or something else, but this I do know, the time I spent in her company were moments of unalloyed happiness. I would have liked a longer visit, but duty calls me away, on taking my departure the Lady invited me to return at my convenience. I found on going to my quarters that Capt. Vittum was about to depart for St. Louis on business connected with the Army. . . .

Thursday, June 18. This morning I wrote a letter to Bro. Samuel. During the day a little excitement was occasioned by Wm. H. Gardner of my Co. and A. J. Shay[1] of Co. "L" having a quarrel which terminated in a fight which resulted in the defeat and rout of Shay, and amusement of those who witnessed the combat. There was nothing more of interest to day. The day was warm and smoky and had indications of rain as a light sprinkle came this afternoon.

1. Private Andrew J. Shay, Branchville, Wis.

Friday, June 19. Having become infatuated of late in reading novels, I occupy my leisure time today by reading a new Novel, the title was the Prairie Flower. This morning cool and signs of rain afternoon some rainy. We drew 17 new horses for our Company this afternoon & for the purpose of supplying new Recruits, and taking the place of horses dead and disabled.

Saturday, June 20. I spent the forenoon a reading. Afternoon I took a ride up in town and out to the fort a half mile south of Rolla. The fort is situated on an eminence commanding the town. Is built in a square shape and constructed of timber with a heavy embankment outside on the north side is a wide entrance and on the four corners of the Parapet are placed 24 pounder Siege guns. Today cool.

Sunday, June 21. I wrote a letter to a friend today, and took a stroll in town. I conclude to give a minute description of the place. As I have mentioned heretofore this is the County Seat of Phelps Co., Mo. The Court House is a brick structure and a credit to the county. There is some fine business houses and Churches, but there has been many new buildings erected for the purpose of trading with troops or in most cases for robing [sic] them of their money as the majority of these places was well stocked with Helljuice, Family disturber, Soldiers delight, Coffin Varnish and many games to take the remaining dimes not spent for the above decoctions. Our Regiment are under marching orders. We drew some saddles tonight for our new Recruits horses. . . .

Monday, June 22. This morning we turned over our old Revolvers of Lafousche[1] pattern and drew new Colts Army Revolvers, a much better Arm. At 9 O'clock our Regiment packed and loaded tents and Camp Equipage and started out on the march again, our destination was Fort Scott, Kansas. Marched 6½ miles and camped at Sicamore Springs 4½ miles west of Rolla. The roads very dusty and day hot. Some sign of rain tonight.

1. The Belgian-made Lefaucheux "pin-fire" 7-mm. revolver.

Tuesday, June 23. At 7 O'clock this morning we resumed our march. Our course was bearing south west on the St. Louis and Springfield R.R. grade. I took command of the advance guard today. We crossed a small stream six times and Big Piney once, after crossing the latter we camped at 3 P.M. marched 16 miles. The day rainy. Not many farms the country by our road was timber and high rocky bluff unsuited for farms.

Wednesday, June 24. The rain fell constantly during the night and did not hold up until noon today. R. S. Hill[1] and T. Beckwith[2] had a fight last night but was stopped before blood was drawn. At 7 O'clock we again took up our march, the road very muddy. At noon we camped at Waynesville, County Seat of Pulaski Co., Mo. on the Gasconade River. Afternoon cloudy and pleasant. The boys are fishing and cooking. *(June 25 is omitted.)*

1. Private Robert G. Hill, Baraboo, Wis., blacksmith.
2. Private Thaddeus Beckwith, Baraboo, Wis.

Friday, June 26. This morning at 7 O'clock we continued our journey and immediately crossed Bear Creek, the roads are very stony and muddy. Some farms under cultivation on our route today and Wheat near the harvest, there was some hills and valleys timbered heavily on our journey. We passed through Lebanon and camped two miles west of the place at noon. Lebanon is the County Seat of Laclede Co., Mo. The place had from appearance once been a thriving town, and some business done here yet. We marched 14 miles today. . . .

Saturday, June 27. . . . We crossed two streams, branches of the Niangua River, and at 1 O'clock P.M. we arrived at Buffalo at which place we camped. I took dinner with a citizen, had a good dinner consisting in part of green peas. We had a heavy shower this afternoon. We marched 26 miles today. Buffalo is a small dilapidated place and the county seat of Dallas Co., Mo.

Sunday, June 28. . . . We crossed the Pomme de Terre River and a number of Creeks this forenoon. Arrived at Bolivar at noon and passed on one mile and camped on the edge of a prairie. The country today was prairie & timber. It rained all the afternoon and we was without shelter, consequently we was wet to the skin. We marched 20 miles. Our Train came up last night. Bolivar is the County Seat of Polk Co., Mo. and as we did not stop at the place I can not give a correct description of it, but somewhat resembled many other towns in the state, in a decayed condition.

Monday, June 29. At 7 O'clock A.M. we again

moved wearily on our road. Our Company was rear guard to our Train. The road was in almost impassable condition, and the Army Mule Whacker frequently resorted to his vocabulary of oaths while urging their long eared beasts through the sea of mud. The country hilly and low land with a plenty of timber. Some farms under good condition. We passed the small town of Fairplay[1] this forenoon. After marching 3 miles west of town our advance guard discovered 16 Bushwhackers who were beating a lively retreat, our boys started in pursuit but lost their game. At 1 P.M. we crossed Bear Creek,[2] at 3 O'clock P.M. we camped at Sac River.[3] The stream was very high. Marched 22 miles. . . .

1. In extreme west central Polk County, Mo.
2. A tributary of Sac River in eastern Cedar County, Mo.
3. From the context this would have to be East Fork or Little Sac River, an eastern tributary of Sac River proper.

Tuesday, June 30. I omitted an incident of yesterday, which I mention here. Joseph H. Doppler[1] of my Company was taken prisoner by guerrillas and his Horse and Equipments, Carbine and Revolver were taken from him and he was allowed to go to his Co. Was captured at Bears Creek, came to Co. last evening. The river keep up, can not cross today, a heavy shower and terrible wind last night. Our Command was Mustered today. Very hot today and signs of rain tonight.

1. Private Joseph H. Doppler, Baraboo, Wis.

Wednesday, July 1. Some rain last night. We remained in camp this foreoon. R. S. Hill of my Co. improved the opportunity by getting very drunk. This afternoon we moved down the river 7 miles to a ferry and camped at sunset. The country along the way was well timbered, some farms and I saw many beautiful springs. Today warm and some cloudy.

Thursday, July 2. This morning we commenced ferrying our Train over Sac River. Capt. Thomas Derry, Co. "L" took Comd of our Cavalry force and we went above the ferry two miles and swam our horses as the stream was deep and turbulent. We continued our course westward two miles and came to West Fork of Sac River[1] which was deep and rapid. While crossing A. D. Kimbal accidentally fell from his horse and he swam out amid the shouts of his comrades. We then continued our journey without further accident and passed through Stockton[2] at 4 O'clock P.M. and camped on a prairie one mile west of town. Stockton is the County Seat of Cedar Co., Mo. and quite a lively place. Marched 9 miles. Today very warm.

1. This would be Sac River proper, a large, northward-flowing tributary of the Osage River, bisecting Dade, Cedar, and southern St. Clair counties. One of several Ozark river names definitely never to take the definite article.

2. Stockton was afterwards burned by Confederate forces.

Friday, July 3. At 6 O'clock this morning we again marched on our way. As we got strung out on the road, my man Kimball gave us another entertainment. His horse became unmanageable by plunging, kicking and running by us at a furious rate, while the symmetrical form of Kimbal was fluttering above the horses back. We crossed a large prairie and through some timber and after a march of 6 miles we came to Cedar Cr.[1] and crossed, and soon after arrived at Horse Creek[2] which we crossed. We continued our wearisome journey until noon when we arrived at Montevallo in Vernon County, Mo. and here we camped, after a march of 20 miles. The day was clear. . . . Lieut. Col. [Richard] White[3] and Capt. [Robert] Carpenter[4] with an Escort started to Fort Scott soon after we camped.

1. A northeast-flowing tributary of Sac River.

2. Another northeast-flowing tributary of Sac River.

3. Richard H. White, Janesville, Wis., one of the regiment's two lieutenant colonels; dismissed Oct. 26, 1863.

4. Robert Carpenter, Sparta, Wis., Captain of Company A. "Capt. Carpenter set the example by wedding the daughter of Dr. Dodge, and now lives in Kansas."—*History of Vernon County*, 392. However, according to Shirley Harris Park, "Mary Elizabeth Dodge [daughter not of Dr. Dodge but of Jonathan Edwards Dodge, Sr., and Phoebe Austin Dodge] married Capt. Robert R. Carpenter on 23 April 1868, after he was discharged 11 Aug. 1865, and settled in Lawrence KS, where he was engaged in the cattle and grain trade [and where he died in 1919 and is buried]. He traveled to Vernon County in the spring of 1868, where he married Mary E. Dodge." It has been stated that these Carpenters settled just northeast of Deerfield after the war, but this is clearly in error.

Saturday, July 4. This morning at sunrise we fired cannon and small arms in honor of our Nations birth or anniversary of her independence. At 6 O'clock A.M. we commenced another weary days march, after a march of 20 miles we arrived at what was once Nevada, the County Seat of Vernon County, Mo., only one or two houses remain to mark the place.[1] We passed on to Little Dry Wood Creek,[2] 7 or 8 miles farther and camped. The day terrible hot.

1. Nevada was burned by Missouri State Militia (Federal) from St. Clair and Cedar counties on May 26. Some 75 houses and all public buildings save the school and the jail were burned.

2. A northward-flowing tributary of the Marmaton River, not far west of Nevada.

Sunday, July 5. This morning at 6 O'clock we start on our way to reach the "Promised Lane" [sic] soon after starting we crossed Big Dry Wood Creek, after a march of 12 miles we camped one mile east of Fort Scott, our journey here ended at 10 O'clock A.M. At 4 O'clock P.M. I went up to the fort and found the place much improved since I last saw it Oct. 2nd 1862. I learn that some Kansas troops who were on duty at the Fort got in a difficulty with the Escort that came in on the 4th with Col. White and Capt. Carpenter and that a lively skirmish ensued 50 or more shots was fired and two Kansas boys was killed and number was wounded, our boys came out of the engagement with one wounded in the hand. Our boys came out victorious. I returned to camp early. A member of Co. "D" was shot through the leg tonight accidentally by a drunken comrade of same Company. . . .

Monday, July 6. Our Company and Co. "A" of our Regiment were ordered to move down to Fort Scott this morning. At 10 O'clock A.M. we pulled up stakes and moved to the Fort, and located our Camp a quarter of a mile south of the Town. The remaining Companies of our Regiment was ordered to move out to Big Dry Wood to engage in outpost duty. Our two Companies were selected for Provost duty in Fort Scott. I took dinner at the Fort Scott Hotel[1] after dinner I put up my tent and arranged the interior for comfort as well as I could with the material I had in hand. Today very hot and this evening there was signs of rain.

1. Located in the former Fort hospital building, now the Historic Site headquarters; also called the Free State Hotel.

Tuesday, July 7. This morning Lieut. Willsey and myself went down in town. The Lieutenant went to the Office of Muster to be mustered as 1st Lieut of our Co. I took a walk in town and found many old acquaintances, all quiet in town. The Kansas troops that had been on duty here are preparing to move to new fields of labor and pastures green. May the Devil play the rogues march when they depart from here. I spent the greater part of the day in town. . . .

Wednesday, July 8. Lieut. Willsey was mustered in yesterday as 1st Lieut. Co. "F" 3rd Wis. Cav and was detailed to serve as Officer of the Day. The morning I was notified to appear at the Office of Muster to be mustered, I was informed that I could not be mustered before the morrow as my papers necessary to complete the muster were not made out. As I was on the idle list I spent the forenoon in town as it was a inviting place for idlers and loafers. . . .

Thursday, July 9. This morning I was Mustered in as 2nd Lieut. Co. "F" 3rd Regt. Wis. Cav. by Major T. J. Weed, Commissary of Muster for the District of Kansas. Muster to date of Commission, date March 20th, 1863. I spent the balance of the day in town, awaiting orders. I saw nothing interesting. . . .

Friday, July 10. I spent the forenoon in camp. At noon I was ordered to join a scouting party of 40 men in command of Capt. Robert Carpenter, our party was of Companies "A" and "F" of our Regt. Our orders were to go in the vicinity of Balltown, Mo. as reports came in that a large number of Bushwhackers was in that locality. We marched on [sic] the direction ordered and the day being extremely hot we took our time so as to keep our horses in good condition. Our course was over prairie principally, and after a journey of 18 miles we camped.

Saturday, July 11. At 7 O'clock this morning we moved forward arrived at Ball Town on the Little Osage River and 22 miles N.E. from Fort Scott at 8 O'clock A.M. We stopped at Doctor Dodges[1] a mile from town and at Doctor Oneals[2] in Balltown to make inquiries about the people and as to the probably locality of the guerrillas. We learned that they had been seen in the woods on the opposite side of the river from town. We immediately commenced the search of the enemy, and after diligent search during the day without results we gave up the hunt and camped at the same place we [sic] last night. Today cloudy and misty.

1. Leonard Dodge, M.D., 59, born Vermont, the oldest child of Rev. N. B. Dodge, superintendent of Harmony Mission. He was the first teacher, first postmaster, first physician and justice of the peace in the neighborhood. "He was brought up in the wilderness and passed his life on the frontier; but he was a gentleman of education and culture, a physician of rare skill and ability, and a man of strict rectitude and morality. . . He was a staunch Union man, never wavering in his devotion to the 'old flag,' but he was of invaluable service to many a Confederate sympathizer, whose property he often saved from conscription or destruction and whose life he often preserved from halter or pistol ball."—*The History of Vernon County, Mo.*, 393.

2. Unidentified. J. T. Neal, M.D., signed an affidavit at Barnesville, Kansas Territory, some 15 miles west, in 1858.

Sunday, July 12. We learn this morning that Capt. [Alexander] Pratt[1] of Co. "F" had been scouting east of Balltown and had an engagement with a guerrilla party of 25 on the farm of Timothy Stearns.[2] Pratt lost one man killed, pierced with five shorts [sic] early in the fight and the enemy had five wounded, and the enemy was soon routed when Pratt pursued and overtook two trying to cross the Osage river when his men fired on them and killed both. We conclude the Knights of the brush convinced themselves that the implacable 3rd Wis. Boys meant business. So they betook themselves to a more congenial locality, which accounts for our fruitless adventure. We started out early to Fort Scott. Arrived in Camp at 1 P.M. Today smoky like unto Indian Summer and nice Breeze.

1. Alexander M. Pratt, Janesville, Wis., captain of Company E, according to the Roster.

2. Timothy W. Stearns was not in the 1860 census. In 1870 he was a farmer in Osage Township, age 43, born Mass.; settled on the Little Osage about a mile downstream from Balltown. Stearns Lake, in Sec. 16, memorializes the family name. A kinswoman, Eliza Stearns, married first Cecil D. Ball (1842), Balltown's founder, then (1863) Robert W. McNeil.

Monday, July 13. Not having any employment today, I resolved to escape the monotonous scenes of camp.[1] So I went out in town where spent the day with jovial companions and at night I attended a Dance got up by the soldiers. Many of the Belles of the Town and vicinity being present made it pleasant and enjoyable, as the party was conducted with decorum, I engaged the company of some young ladies present and danced a few sets, and spent a little time in pleasant conversation. At 11 P.M. I went to camp and retired for sleep. The day was very warm.

1. Reportedly the Federal camp at Balltown lay just northeast of town, on the right or south bank of the Little Osage, a spot subject to flooding, as they shortly learned.

Tuesday, July 14. There was nothing interesting in camp this morning so I walked out in town. I learn that Gen. Blunt and his force had lately had a terrific engagement with the Rebel Genl. [Douglas] Coopers[1] command at Fort Gibson C. N.[2] resulting in the defeat of the enemy with heavy loss. I did not learn our loss. I spent the forenoon in town and the afternoon I spent in camp. All quiet with us.

1. Brigadier General Douglas H. Cooper, commander 1st Regiment Choctaw and Chickasaw Mounted Rifles.
2. Cherokee Nation.

Wednesday, July 15. This forenoon I was in town, but I found nothing very interesting to make mention of. Afternoon I wrote a letter to Bro. Samuel. This evening Capt. Vittum arrived in camp from St. Louis looking well and happy. I was in town this evening and learned that the 13th Kans. Regt would take their departure on the morrow for Arkansas. I saw the Colonel and Officers in a Saloon as I passed down street, and I came to the conclusion that an all night carouse had fairly begun as drinking was freely indulged in and song singing, and all hands were boisterous. . . .

Thursday, July 16. I spent the day in camp. There was nothing in camp very interesting, Capt. Carpenter took command of a scouting party today, and started out to Missouri to disturb the quiet retreat of the Devils Battalions whose advent in our locality they find, not so comfortable. There was two dances in Fort Scott tonight, one of which I attended, and enjoyed the few hours I remained there. I returned to camp at midnight. It was raining at the time. . . .

Friday, July 17. The clouds was bottom side up this morning, consequently the rain came upon us like unto a torrent, and our camp was an unenviable abode. We wished those fellows who had an occasion to go to Canada had mistaken the route and was at this time standing at our tent door like the Devil at Heavens gate begging for admission, we think our reply would be to go to that place prepared for you. The rain continued all day, and we continued in our tents. . . .

Saturday, July 18. This forenoon Corporal H. J. Gardner,[1] Privates A. Pettys [2]and Thos. Chambers [3] left here on furlough to Wisconsin. There was nothing farther to chronicle only our Camp presented the appearance of a wash day, as clothing, blankets, &c was hung out in promiscuous abundance to dry on account of yesterdays rain. I remained in camp today. . . .

1. Corporal Hiram J. Gardner, Baraboo, Wis.
2. Private Amos Pettis, Reedsburg, Wis.
3. Private Thomas Chambers, Baraboo, Wis.

Sunday, July 19. This day I spent in camp. C. H. Blodgett[1] returned to Company from Leavenworth Hospital where he had been sick. Daniel Wright[2] returned from furlough, and Capt. Carpenter came in from scout. He reported no guerrillas could be found, nothing farther to relate today. Today very warm.

1. Private Carlton H. Blodgett, Janesville, Wis., saddler.
2. Private Daniel A. Wright, Ironton, Wis.

Monday, July 20. This forenoon I remained in camp. At 2 O'clock P.M. I took command of 25 men to escort a Capt. Crawford and Lieut. to Greenfield, Mo.[1] 65 miles distant. I learned they belonged to a Kans. Regt. We camped at Peter Browns[2] place on Big Dry Wood, 12 miles from Fort Scott. Today very warm.

1. Seat of Dade County, Mo.
2. Perhaps Peter Brown, 34, born in Ohio.

Tuesday, July 21. At 5 O'clock this morning we resumed our journey, which took us over a vast prairie. We suffered for want of water. During the afternoon we came upon some troops 45 or 50 in number whom we supposed to be a large guerrilla party when we first discovered them. I immediately put my men in position for action and then I rode forward to enquire who they were. I soon learned they were a portion of the 2nd Kans. Cavy. We continued our journey and camped at a widow Hedges[1] place on Horse Creek. Marched 35 miles today. Today very hot.

1. Unidentified.

Wednesday, July 22. We started at 5 O'clock this morning and soon crossed Horse Creek, passed through timber, and over prairie and after a march of 18 miles we arrived at Greenfield at 9 O'clock A.M. We took breakfast and led our horses after which I looked over the town, this being the county seat of Dade Co., Mo. and a very beautiful place. At 11

O'clock A.M. we started on our way back to Fort Scott, marched two miles and camped. Some rain this morning. Day very hot.

Thursday, July 23. Having rested ourselves and horses yesterday, I took up the march to Fort Scott at 6½ O'clock A.M. our journey being mostly over prairie, and our canteens not being sufficient to carry the necessary supply water, we suffered exceedingly with thirst, dust and heat the morning was cloudy but cleared away and the day became sultry and oppressive. Marched 43 miles today and camped on Little Dry Wood.

Friday, July 24. We had a heavy shower early this morning. At 7½ O'clock A.M. we resumed our journey, and after a march of 20 miles we arrived at Fort Scott at 4 P.M. Corpl Simonds[1] of my Co. was obliged to leave his horse at Dry Wood as it was unable to go farther. This evening a terrific shower visited us accompanied with constant thunder & lightning, and terrible wind throwing our tents in a confused mass over the ground and exposing us to the fury of the storm.

1. Corporal Norman Simonds, Baraboo, Wis.

Saturday, July 25. I spent the day in town and joined some jolly companions in a few games for amusement. At 8 O'clock P.M. Companies "A" and "F" of our Regt had orders to move without unnecessary delay to Ball Town and establish an Outpost there. At

10 P.M. our two companies moved out towards Missouri. Today very warm.

Sunday, July 26. We marched all last night, had a dark night and quite an amount of trouble with the men, as many of them had imbibed too freely of Fort Scott "Benzine and Turpentine." Early this forenoon we arrived at Ball Town, on arriving two shots was fired at us from the opposite side of the Little Osage river, no harm done. This afternoon the guerrillas concluded to make our position uncomfortable so they opened a lively fusillade upon us, when we soon gave them to understand that we came here to do a little of that kind of work, which was kept up with but little intermission during the afternoon. We had two horses slightly wounded but no other casualty with us. We think some of the enemy killed. Today pleasant.

Monday, July 27. Our camp guard heard sawing and hammering in the enemies domain during the night, and our conclusions are that we sent some of them to dine and lodge with their prototype, his (Satanic Majesty). The Osage though narrow was very deep and bank full could not be crossed with safety on horses so we constructed a raft this morning and a number of us crossed over and scouted the country near by but found no enemy, but found considerable blood which indicated that our shots had been a little to effectual for comfort, but we was unable to learn true results, but think the hammering &c was caused in preparing a coffin or boxes for burying some of their number. After I returned to camp I walked up to the residence of Josiah Austin[1] near by. I spent a few hours there very pleasant with his two widow-sisters and four amiable nieces. I took dinner with the family which was worthy of more praise than I have at command to bestow upon it. I fear that I forgot all rules of propriety, and gave cause for my good friend to suspect I had been on a protracted fast. I returned to camp in due time, found all quiet today. Today very pleasant.

1. "Josiah Miller Austin was an elder and a lay preacher of the church in Little Osage. As a young man, he attended Hanover College, a Presbyterian school in Hanover, Ind. When the husbands of his sisters (Phebe Dodge and Sarah Elizabeth Garrison) died at Nevada City, Cal., in 1851, Josiah broke his engagement to be married in order to help his sisters and their combined nine children."—Shirley Harris Park. Josiah, 48, born in Vermont, was the son of Daniel H. Austin, millwright of Harmony Mission, who also built the mill at Balltown. In 1836 father and son "settled half a mile east of Balltown." On May 6, 1998, the editor visited and confirmed the site, ½ mile northwest of Balltown Cemetery, SWSE18-37-32, now a conspicuous eminence in a plowed field, marked only by scattered bits of broken crockery, china, glassware, hand-wrought iron objects, brassware, etc.

Tuesday, July 28. I spent the greater portion of the day in camp. We think our gallant Knights of the brush who displayed much fine talent in selecting us for cowards found to their sorrow that we mean business. So they have come to the conclusion that it is folly to waste ammunition on us and have gone where their carcasses are not so liable to become a lead mine. We enjoy a quiet today. I took a walk up to Mr. Austins this afternoon where I enjoyed a little visit with our new made friends. Some indications of rain.

Wednesday, July 29. I remained in camp this forenoon. Afternoon I became weary of the scenes of camp, I concluded to spend the afternoon more refined society, so I again sought the company of the ladies on the hill where pure happiness can always be found. On returning to camp I learned by some of the boys who had been to the Fort that Wm. H. Gardner was shot twice in the forehead and killed by Capt. Tuff a scout, last evening in a quarrel.[1] Today warm.

1. Fort Scott newspapers unlocated for this date.

Thursday, July 30. This morning early I saddled my horse preparatory to going on a scout. I joined Capt. Carpenter and 30 men of our Squadrons and marched northward 15 miles to the Marais des Cygnes River[1] where we came upon a party of Bushwhackers 10 in number who were quartered in an old house. We charged upon them and killed two of their number, the balance escaped in the brush. We captured 6 horses and equipments, 4 guns and 6 revolvers, some Blankets and clothing besides some camp equipage which the enemy left in their great haste to escape the inevitable destruction that was coming upon them. We concluded that they was on the eve of their departure on a long journey as they had a large quantity of meal cooked, and a large kettle-full cooking in the house beside a quantity of corn bread baked which we destroyed. We decided to return to camp after we had satisfied ourselves that the enemy was no longer in this locality. We returned to camp arriving at sunset after a march of 36 miles. . . .

1. Marais des Cygnes ("Marsh of the Swans"), the upper Big Osage River, flows east out of Kansas, through Bates County, joining the Marmaton-Little Osage to form the Big Osage proper.

Friday, July 31. This morning Lieut. Willsey, Sergt. M. E. Waite and other departed to Fort Scott. I remained in camp this forenoon. Afternoon Capt. Carpenter wished me to accompany him up to the house on the hill. I did so, and soon we found ourselves engaged in pleasant conversation with the Misses, Martha, Mary, and Ellen Dodges,[1] and Miss Emaline Garrison[2] and their good old Mothers. [3] We became very much interested in conversation and did not realize that time had made our long stay some short until we was summoned to set down to a fine prepared supper. I will omit entering into a description of what was spread before us, but we imagined ourselves (Capt. and self) at our Old Mothers table and filling our hungry stomachs. Suffice it to say we could not have been better entertained. After supper Capt. and self returned to camp, much pleased with our visit. All quiet in our neighborhood. I find nothing more to relate of today. Only the day was pleasant.

1. Martha L., 25, Mary E., 23, and H. Ellen, 16, all born in Missouri.

2. Sarah Emaline Garrison, 20.

3. Phoebe (Feba, Phebe) Dodge, 45, born in Vermont, and Sarah Elizabeth Garrison, 40, born in 1822 at Harmony Mission.

Saturday, August 1. This forenoon I was idle. I could hardly find any process by which to expel the lassitude that soon takes possession of one self when off duty and compelled to remain in camp idle. This afternoon I contented myself reading, while the boys sought excitement in various games. Since camping here we have been able to procure good rations, such as green corn, green beans, new Potatoes, cucumbers, Onions, and green apples. Many of the boys are sick with Ague, bilious fever, and malarious complaints so we have an effective force of only 80 men out of 200. There is report that the guerrilla bands contemplate a combined attack on us. We say let them combine, and let them attack, we will remain while they as on former occasions take a sudden idea that some other locality is more congenial to their happiness. Today very warm.

Sunday, August 2. This morning Capt. Carpenter took 30 men and proceeded on a scout, returned soon after noon. They saw two guerrillas but could not reach them as they was making good their escape. There was some rain this afternoon. Capt. Carpenter and myself spent the evening with the ladies on the hill. Day very warm.

Monday, August 3. We spent the day in Camp. There was nothing important transpired in Camp. The day very warm. This evening Capt. Carpenter and myself resolved to surprise a camp of Bushwhackers near Nevada, soon after dark we had 30 men of our Companies ready and anxious to start, besides 10 regular government Scouts. We left camp immediately, observing our course by the wind as the night was dark and our direction was over prairie and no road, until we reached the Marmaton River, this we found bank full, and the depth 40 feet. It looked like a desperate undertaking to cross, but we succeed in crossing without accident and continued on to Nevada, arrive there at 2 O'clock in the night and stopped at the house[1] of Captain Taylor a leader of a guerrilla party. We was wet to our waist and chilly, so we remained until morning.

1. William Henry Taylor's house in Nevada had been burned with the rest of the town by Federal militia in May, says *The History of Vernon County*, 317.

Tuesday, August 4. At daylight we started back, we was now 12 miles from Camp. We scouted the woods early this morning and came upon the camp of the enemy near Marmaton river where they had left their meat cooking and bread for breakfast, besides leaving their coats and blankets, these we burnt as they was infested with a colony that we had on former occasions been quite familiar with. We now became satisfied that the guerrillas had heard us coming and they fled hastily in the woods. We commenced a hunt and soon we had them fleeing wildly in the woods, but could not see them the undergrowth being so dense, but finally we lost their direction, and being very warm and thirsty we went in search of water at the residence of Mr. Ellis[1] nearby and while there two of the enemy who had become separated from their party rode near the house and the boys fired upon them killing one whose name we learned was Wm. Godfrey[2] the other by name Jas. Brooks[3] escaped with all the speed his horse could make. I ran out and secured Godfreys horse and double barrel gun. While securing the horse 30 guerrillas in command of Bill Marchbanks[4] fired on me without harm and then fled. Godfrey was hit in seven places with Carbine bullets. We immediately pursued the enemy and not being able to find them and learning they had gone from here, we concluded to return to camp as both men and horses was nearly exhausted. Arrived in Camp at sunset. The day was terrible warm.

1. William J. Ellis, 51, native of Tennessee, farmed in Section 17, Washington Township, with wife Elizabeth and 4 grown or teen children.

2. William Godfrey, 47, born in Kentucky.

3. Unidentified.

4. William Marchbanks, 27, in 1861 was commissioned captain in the Missouri State Guard. After Pea Ridge he returned home with authority to recruit and became Vernon County's most prominent Bushwhacker leader. "The Federals who fought him generally respect him."—*The History of Vernon County,* 335.

Wednesday, August 5. The boys spent the day in camp in pursuit of various amusements. I spent this forenoon resting, as last night I did not get the rest required. I took a walk with Capt. Carpenter this afternoon we stopped in to see the neighbors on the hill, took supper with them after which we engaged in conversation with the ladies on various topic, during which we discovered the family was good Presbyterians, the older portion was missionaries among the Osage Indians here years gone by.[1] We returned to camp at 9 O'clock P.M. The day was very warm.

1. A reference to Harmony Mission, established in southern Bates County in 1821. At the breakup of the Mission in the late 1820s many of the Mission families moved upriver to the Balltown or Little Osage settlement.

Thursday, August 6. Last night at 1 O'clock our camp was all in readiness for an attach as a messenger came in from one of the Picket posts and reported that about 50 guerrillas was seen near them but soon went away. A sharp look out was kept until day, but no attack was made. Capt. Carpenter went to Fort Scott this morning. I remained in camp all day. There was some indications of rain, but little came. Today warm and quiet. Captain Carpenter and others came in camp this evening. Day warm.

Friday, August 7. This morning Capt. Carpenter with 30 men went on another scout, after a day of fruitless adventure they returned to camp at sunset. Lieut [J. B.] Pond[1] of Co. "C" and a portion of his Co. Capt. Shaw of Co. "D" and a portion of his Co. besides some Kans. troops accompanied him making our available force to night about 175 men. I remained in command of camp today. The day was very warm.

1. James B. Pond, Janesville, Wis., captain of Company C.

Saturday, August 8. This morning I went in company with Capt. Carpenter and 100 men on an expedition near Montevallo on Clear Creek.[1] At about sunset we came upon a small party of guerrillas and fired on them without any definite results only hastening their retreat, our attention was soon turned on two of the number on foot, I captured one and Joe Ury[2] a Scout the other, they were brothers and named Pryor,[3] captured them on Clear Creek, Mo. We became satisfied that they was guerrillas so they was turned over to the tender mercies of Joe Ury and his blood thirsty companions 10 in number who soon sent them to a warmer climate. We camped soon after, marched 35 miles. Today quite warm.

1. Clear Creek rises in Barton County and flows north-northeast through southeast Vernon County, entering the Osage River in southwest St. Clair County.

2. Josiah C. Ury, "a famous Federal scout and spy," was a son of Lewis L. Ury, "a strong Union man" whose house stood where modern Garland, Kan., stands.

3. "George and Lafayette Prior were killed at their home on Clear Creek, in section 16, by a detachment of Federals under Lieut. Pond, of the 3d Wisconsin. Both were young men. George had been for a time in the Confederate army, but at the time they were killed the boys were generally deemed harmless, although the Federals said they were bushwhackers."—*The History of Vernon County, Mo.*, 847.

Sunday, August 9. We had breakfast and started early. Lieut. Pond who had accompanied us took 40 men and started on another direction from us. After scouting the woods on Clear Creek this forenoon we took a west course 8 miles and camped on Pleasant run[1] a branch of Little Dry Wood, here we took supper. Lieut. Pond came in and reported a guerrilla camp on Clear Creek. We immediately started on our way to surround and capture the camp the night was to dark for us to succeed. So we camped. Day cloudy and rain.

1. Pleasant Run rises near modern Sheldon, Mo., and flows northwest into Little Drywood Creek in northern Drywood Township.

Monday, August 10. We found we was one mile from the camp we was in search of but could not find Lieut. Pond and Command so we concluded to make the attack alone. We advanced as quiet as circumstances would admit of and dashed upon the camp which contained one man who was asleep at the time but made his escape through a shower of bullets. We captured 5 horses and equipments, some camp equipage of little value, the horses are good. We conclude the remainder of the party are on a plundering expedition. We went in search of Lieut. Pond and found him and men at a widows house. We prepared and eat breakfast here after which we went back to Pleasant River where we scouted during the afternoon without discovering an enemy, a little before night a heavy shower came upon us, otherwise the day was pleasant. Camped 6 miles south of Nevada.

Tuesday, August 11. This morning we decided to return to camp as farther search for the terror stricken Bushwhacks we regard as useless, they having retired to haunts of Bats, Owls and kindred spirits. We scouted the country on our way to camp to make sure that no foe was in our neighborhood. Arrived at camp at 2 O'clock P.M. The day was very warm. I was invited to spend the evening at Mr. Austins on the hill, I did not hesitate to accept the invitation, and was pleased with my visit.

Wednesday, August 12. On returning to camp last evening, I learn that Lieut. Willsey went to Fort Scott Hospital sick on the 9th inst. leaving me in command of Company. This morning Capt. Carpenter with our Scouts Joe Ury, Frank Lonacre,[1] Sam Coens,[2] Jas Harrington[3] and others went to Fort Scott. I was left in command of camp. The boys got up a dance this evening and brought in the ladies of the neighborhood to join them in the festivities of the evening, and all passed a pleasant evening, and the ladies complimented me for the gentlemanly conduct of the men. I spent a portion of the evening with the ladies on the hill. Day quite warm.

1. W. F. Longacre, 38, a farmer in Drywood Township, known to be hospitable to Federal troops. Andrew J. Longacre, 33, likewise a farmer in Drywood Township, presumably his brother, in 1861 was 2nd Lt., Co. E, 7th Cavalry Regiment 8th Division, Missouri State Guard (i.e. pro-Confederate).

2. Unidentified.

3. Unidentified.

Thursday, August 13. There was nothing transpired with us unusual today, the boys seem to have run out to the end of their catalogue of amusements last evening at the dance; and today our camp has been one of unusual quiet. We are anxious to learn what our Army is doing in other places or departments.

Friday, August 14. The boys have concluded to adopt more refined amusements than has been their custom. This morning quite a number of the boys was again preparing for another dance to take place at a room in our camp and as a consequence they was quite busy engaging the neighbor Ladies to assist in making the program complete for this evening. I became weary of my camp confinement, so I thought a more congenial place to spend the afternoon could not be found, than with the Ladies on the hill, where I spent a few hours pleasantly. On returning to camp I found the boys bringing in the Ladies for the dance. Capt. Carpenter returned from the Fort this evening. Day very warm.

Saturday, August 15. The dance was continued through the night with good order, and closed at daylight this morning. I was not busy today. The camp presents the usual degree of quiet, many of our men are sick with Ague[1] and fevers and kindred diseases produced by miasmic poison. Doctor Leonard Dodge a citizen living nearby has been employed to attend to our sick. We sent out a few men on a scout this evening, no enemy near they report. One of the scouts was hurt by horse falling on him. Day very warm.

1. Malaria, "the most universal and ever present disease [on the frontier]," was called intermittent fever, congestive fever, the ague (from "acute," pronounced *A-gew*), or bilious fever.—Everett Dick, *The Dixie Frontier,* Knopf, 1948, 221.

Sunday, August 16. This morning at the usual hour I attended church at a School House[1] near Camp. Mr. Austin our neighbor preached the sermon, the Text was 2nd Timothy, 4th Chapt, 7th and 8th verses, after services good old Lady Dodge of the mansion on the hill, invited one to accompany them home and take dinner. I accepted and had a good dinner, and a pleasant afternoon with the young ladies. . . .

1. "The first school house was a log building put up in 1835 on the Osage, near Balltown, by Wm. Modrel, D. H. Austin and others. The first teacher here is thought to have been Dr. Leonard Dodge, but this is not certain. This building was also used as a church, until a frame building was put up for religious and school purposes, in about 1839 or 1840."—*The History of Vernon County, Mo.*, 158. Emma Stearns Wood (1833-1926) attended the school while living at Balltown with her mother, 1843-47; she described it as a bare 25 feet wide, standing beside the cemetery "with not a tree to break the wind." Most of the students came and went on horseback. Emma had praise for the teachers, college-educated New Englanders.

Monday, August 17. There was a Scouting party went out from our camp last evening and returned this morning and brought with them an old Rebel sympathizer and after a preliminary examination we decided that he was unsafe to be allowed his liberty so we sent the old traitor to Fort Scott for imprisonment and await trial before a military tribunal. I sent the of any [sic] Company to Fort Scott Hospital for treatment as they had been very sick since the 13th inst. Their names was E. H. Rogers,[1] Oscar Allen, and Geo. R. Kelly.[2] There was another scouting party in command of Lieut. [George] Ellis[3] of Co. "A" went out of camp today. Today very warm.

1. Private Edward H. Rodgers, Janesville, Wis.

2. Corporal Kelly was killed by Bushwhackers Oct. 10, 1863.

3. George M. Ellis, Sheldon, Wis., second lieutenant in Company A.

Tuesday, August 18. This morning some of our Govt Scouts was ordered to report to Fort Scott Hd. Qrs. for duty at other places. More of our men have been added to the sick list today, our force for duty is diminishing every day by sickness which puts a heavy duty on the well men. The day has been very hot and oppressive.

Wednesday, August 19. Lieut. Ellis and command came in the morning, brought two young men who gave their names as Duncan[1] & Newman[2] they was supposed to be Knights of the brush and was accordingly sent to Fort Scott for imprisonment and trial. We gained secret information today, that a party of guerrillas lead by one Pony Hill[3] would camp to night at a spot near the Marais des Cygnes river. As we delight to make the abode of these spirits of the damned very uncomfortable, Lieut. Ellis and myself with about 20 men obtained orders to proceed to the place and if possible annihilate them. We got possession of the signals of this band, which they used when about to camp, that others of their party in the woods might know of their coming. After dark we left camp and hastened to the spot, arriving in time as the party we was after arrived soon after, and before camping they gave three whoops imitating the Owl which we answered by the Whippoorwill. They came on and camped a quarter of mile from us. We decided to keep quiet and not make attack until a late hour. About midnight we left a sufficient guard with our horses while we proceed on foot through a dense undergrowth of vines and brush to attack the enemy. Lieut. Ellis and myself took the lead while our men came up in rear of us. We came upon the camp and discovered the leader Pony Hill standing by his horse, when the Lieut. and myself each fired at him, but he escaped in the brush. His party being asleep then awoke and followed their leaders example, but two of their number was soon sleeping their last sleep while their more fortunate comrades escaped. We captured 9 horses and equipments, some guns and Revolvers, besides Pony Hills Sharps rifle, fine boots, and horse. The night being very dark we deemed farther search unnecessary and returned to our horses, where we remained until morning light. The day was very warm. Night cool.

1. Unidentified.
2. Likely J. N. Newman, 38, a farmer in Osage Township.

3. The notorious "Pony" Hill was probably James N. Hill, 28, a farmer in Osage Township.

Thursday, August 20. At an early hour we started to camp, and made the trip in due time. I spent a good portion of the day in camp, but during the afternoon I spent an hour on the hill with the Ladies who I have found very pleasant and agreeable and I have found it a pleasant place to escape the sameness of camp which to me is tiresome, beyond my capacity to endure very long. The day was very warm.

Friday, August 21. I spent the day in camp. I was suffering with a severe headache all day. We gained information that some guerrillas was in the habit of visiting two families living on Muddy Creek,[1] north of us 9 or 10 miles. So I was ordered to take a sufficient number of men and secrete ourselves at these houses and arrest any that approached. We started on the expedition at dark and in a short time arrived at the places designated and soon after we had located ourselves we found that we was elected to fight Mosquitoes and fleas innumerable as they assailed our position. We remained until day and searched the houses, found none but women and children, we returned to camp by way of Priors Creek.[2] The day quite warm.

1. A small eastward-flowing tributary of the Marmaton River, in south central Bates County, Mo.

2. Pryor Creek rises in southwest Bates County and flows southeast, entering the Little Osage River near present Metz, Mo.

Saturday, August 22. We arrived in camp at 11 O'clock A.M. We did not meet with any success on our expedition. We was about two miles from camp. Daniel Wright of my Company became thirsty and apprehending no danger he went in search of water. John F. Greening[1] another member of my Co. was out of camp hunting a horse and discovered Wright and supposed he was a lone bushwhacker, he charge on him, Wright saw him coming, supposed Greening was a bushwhack he fired a shot at him at long range and fled hastily to camp and Greening pursued him with all the speed possible until he discovered his mistake. This little incident was enjoyed by us, but poor Wright was doomed to perpetual jests and jokes of the company for his lack of bravery. Today very warm.

1. Private John F. Greening, Baraboo, Wis.

Monday, August 24. I slept very cold last night, there was some frost visible this morning, fire was a comfortable luxury today as the day was cloudy and cold. Capt. Carpenter and some of the boys went to Fort Scott this morning. I stayed in camp nearly all day, but I took a respite of two hours in visiting my Lady friends on the hill, where as usual I found all at peace with man, and they claim to be with their Maker. I consider this household worthy all the respect due all amiable and christian ladies. Some of the boys went out to Pony Hills house this evening to capture him if there, but had no success.

Tuesday, August 25. My duty was necessary in camp as I was in command of the camp in the absence of Capt. Carpenter. I admitted a few men to go out hunting today, in which they killed a large number of squirrels which supplied our table with fresh meat. Captain Carpenter and his 1st Lieut [John] Davis[1] and some of the boys returned from the Fort this morning. The Capt. took all the men he could raise out of our Companies and at 11 O'clock this evening started in the direction of Papinsville on a Scout. No other incident worthy of mention. Today cool.

1. John Davis, Leon, Wis., first lieutenant in Company A.

Wednesday, August 26. I remained in camp nearly all day towards evening I was invited to Mr. Austins to eat melons. I accepted and was soon surrounded with millifluence of melon juice and sweet voices of ladies. I soon found myself involved in a frolic with the young ladies in washing their faces while they gave me a pelting with melon rinds. I enjoyed myself and the ladies took the jokes kindly. At about 12 O'clock tonight our Picket was fired at by four guerrillas who escaped without doing injury. Today pleasant.

Thursday, August 27. Today some rainy, very cloudy but otherwise pleasant. I spent a portion of the day writing to Bro. Samuel and Sister Cornelia. Our Camp was very quiet owing to our small number.

Friday, August 28. I spent the day in camp at

various duties that pertain to our profession. I was reading some tracts left in Camp by some one which may be beneficial to my spiritual welfare. Capt. Carpenter and men returned from Scout this afternoon and reports the Bushwhackers as having gone to h--l for recruits and general orders from his Satanic Majesty. They did not see any of the enemy and having scouted over quite an extent of country without being able to run on to any, it is supposed they must be called in to replenish. Today quite pleasant.

Saturday, August 29. I tried to content myself with what might fall to my lot this day. I attribute the monotony that follows a stay in camp to be the sole cause of many rough jokes that call the attention of officers to put a stop to. As a substitute I seek relief in the Company of my new made friends on the hill. Capt. Carpenter and myself and a few men of the Companies who were singers went to spend the evening with the ladies at Mr. Austins and practice singing. We had a good time and was pleasantly entertained by the ladies. Today cool.

Sunday, August 30. This morning early I took command of 30 men detailed from Companies "A" and "F" 3rd Wis. Cav. and 7 Wagons and Teams and started after corn in Bates Co. 20 miles distant. Our route took us over a large prairie, the Marais des Cygnes river and Miami.[1] We arrived at our destination at sunset, on arriving at the place I discovered some women with a team hauling corn away I ordered them to remain with us that no information could be carried to the enemy. While I was thus engaged, a scout by the name of John White[2] ran on to a party of bushwhack 6 in number at an old house. One by name of Abraham Blankenbaker[3] tried to escape and White shot and killed him the others escaped. One who was the leader by name Sam. Potter[4] was husband of a woman I had compelled to return with wagon. . . .

1. Miami Creek, in southwestern Bates County, rises in Kansas and flows eastward into the Marais des Cygnes River.

2. Unidentified.

3. Unidentified.

4. Samuel Potter, 43, a laborer in Lone Oak Township, Bates County (Papinsville vicinity).

Monday, August 31. This morning early we loaded our wagons, and had breakfast, after which I released my prisoners, Sam Potters wife and two Miss Dempseys.[1] I then started to Balltown or camp. On arriving at the Marais des Cygnes river my advance guard was fired into by 75 guerrillas who was secreted on the opposite bank of the river. Silas Davis[2] of Co. "A" was shot through the body and killed and 4 wounded of same Co. One by name of Jacob Farber[3] was wounded in nine places. I immediately took what men I could muster and charged the enemy and killed three and wounded some who escaped with their comrades on our approach. I cared for my wounded, and poor Davis I placed in a wagon and resumed my journey unmolested. We arrived in Camp at sunset and placed the wounded in good quarters. Day hot.

1. Probably daughters of Patrick C. Dempsey, 53, a farmer in Pleasant Gap Township, Bates County. He boasted 6.
2. Listed in the Roster as Pvt. Josiah Davis, Sparta, Wis.
3. Private Jacob Ferber, Madison, Wis.

Tuesday, September 1. Our wounded are doing well as can be expected. Doctor Dodge was busy during the night dressing their wounds. I found more of my boys escaped with ball holes through their cloths, and my horse was shot through the top of neck and one bullet passed through my hat near the crown, in yesterdays frolic. This morning I made coffin for Davis while the boys were making necessary preparations for the burial. At 2 O'clock P.M. I took command of the funeral escort and we proceeded slowly to the burial of our comrade Silas Davis. We buried him with due Military honors at a small cemetery at the School House near Balltown. A large number of civilians was present. After the burial we returned to camp where I dismissed the escort. After a short stay in camp I went up to Mr. Austins and had a pleasant chat with the family for the space of two hours. . . .

For 17 days Porter wrote only of routine, camp housekeeping, etc.

Saturday, September 19. This morning Capt. Carpenter and Lt. Willsey and a few men went on a scout towards Nevada. They ran onto four guerrillas near Marmaton river but failed to capture or kill any as they made good their escape. But our boys succeeded in capturing one of their horses belonging to Albert Dickinson[1] one of the guerrillas. I superintended the hauling of Plank for fortifying our camp. There was nothing more worthy of mention with us today. . . .

1. Probably Albert Dickerson, 22, a neighbor of James N. "Pony" Hill.

Sunday, September 20. I attended church at the usual hour this morning. Mr. Austin delivered a good sermon to a large and attentive audience. This evening Sergt Luce[1] of my Co. and myself went on the hill to spend the evening with the young ladies, we had a pleasant visit. Today very pleasant.

1. Sergeant Leonard P. Luce, Cazenovia, Wis., afterwards lieutenant.

Monday, September 21. I spent the day in camp was not engaged at any duty of consequence. Some of the boys are out foraging and others are performing various duties in camp. We are arranging for fortifying our camp on the most exposed sides as a protection against guerrillas picking off our men from the brush. Today pleasant.

Tuesday, September 22. I wrote a letter to a friend in Wis. this forenoon. This afternoon I accompanied Capt. Carpenter and Frank Longacre a Scout on a reconnoitre on Priors and Muddy creeks we did not make any near discoveries, so we headed toward camp where we arrived at 9 O'clock P.M. Day pleasant.

Wednesday, September 23. This forenoon I remained in camp and as usual I was not contented to remain without something exciting to keep life running smoothly, and disease a long way off. Afternoon Leonard P. Luce, Simeon Davis,[1] Augustus Brooks with an ambulance and myself engaged the company of the Misses W. F. Dodge,[2] M. L. Dodge, H. E. Dodge, and S. E. Garrison and went out three miles north to a large Peach Orchard where we procured a large supply of the delicious fruit, and had a pleasant time with our lady friends who expressed themselves as well pleased with the novelty of this afternoon excursion. . . .

1. Corporal Simeon Bennett Davis, Ironton, Wis. He afterwards (1866) married Sarah Emaline Garrison.

2. Should read M. E. Dodge (for Mary Elizabeth); apparently a transcriber's error.

From Sept. 24 to Oct. 6 Porter wrote only of routine and boredom. "We think a few Bushwhacks could make themselves useful as well as obnoxious in these parts at this time, by stimulating us to action and furnishing us exciting employment," he wrote on Oct. 2. On Sept. 28 the "citizenry of Balltown" sent a four-page petition to Gen. James G. Blunt, requesting that a company of the 3rd Wisconsin Cavalry "be allowed to remain" to protect the community from the recent fate of Lawrence, Kansas.

Wednesday, October 7. This morning early we

received orders to move to Fort Scott without delay. The bearer of the Dispatch stated that a dispatch came in the Fort before he left from Baxter Springs[1] stating that Genl Blunt and escort had been attacked by Quantrell and his band of merciless cutthroats numbering 600 men or devils, and a terrible slaughter of our troops had taken place at Baxter yesterday. We packed tents and equipage but transportation being insufficient, we left a portion with a detail of troops, and Companies "A" and "F" soon moved out on the road to Fort Scott. After a warm and dusty march we arrived at the Fort at 8 O'clock P.M. Soon after our arrival Capt. Carpenter and 20 men was ordered to return to Balltown at once.

1. In Cherokee County, in extreme southeast Kansas.

Thursday, October 8. This morning Genl Blunt and command arrived at Fort Scott bringing Major [H. Z.] Curtis[1] and Lieut. [Asa] Farr[2] who were killed at Baxter. Major Curtis was son of Genl. Curtis[3] and Lieut. Farr was Regt. Quarter Master of 3rd. Wis. Cav. and at the time they were killed, belonged on Genl. Blunts Staff. Our Regt. Band was with Blunt and all killed. M. Bulow[4] of my company belonged to the band and was killed. Co. "I" of our Regt. was the Generals Body Guard and lost many men, besides many were killed who belonged to other Companies. This afternoon I was ordered with 6 men to make a reconnoiter on Dry Wood. I did so, and returned at 10 P.M.

1. Major H. Z. Curtis, assistant adjutant general.
2. Asa W. Farr, Geneva, Wis., regimental quartermaster.
3. Major General Samuel R. Curtis, the victor of Pea Ridge, commanded the Federal Department of Missouri, including Kansas from the fall of 1862.
4. Private Heinrich Beulow, Baraboo, Wis., bugler.

After several days' duty as Officer of the Picket at Fort Scott, Porter rejoined his company at Balltown.

Saturday, October 17. This morning at 4 O'clock I was ordered to take command of 20 men of Companies "A" and "F" of my Regt. and join Colonel Lions of the 9th Kansas Cavalry who had just arrived with a number of Cav. Companies and was in pursuit of the Confederate Colonels Shelby[1] and Coffee[2] who had made a raid in Missouri with a force of 600 men. We took a southerly direction on starting out, soon after sunrise our rear guard was fired into by guerrillas when our boys gave them a little of the same medicine which killed two instantly, and the remainder fled. We kept on our way to Nevada and fed our horses. We then took a south east course 14 miles from Shanghai[3] and halted to feed our horses at sunset and take a little Hard-tack and raw bacon ourselves. At 10 O'clock P.M. Brig. Genl. Ewing and Col. Wm. Weer came up with a force and joined us, making our force 1700 men. We then started in the direction of Carthage. Day cool.

1. Joseph O. Shelby, afterwards Brigadier General. This was his famous raid on Marshall, Mo., in which he was ably seconded by Vernon County's Colonel DeWitt Clinton Hunter,

who led the retreat of, and saved, half the command, described as "one of the best managed movements of the war."—*The History of Vernon County, Mo.*, 329.

2. John T. Coffee (1816-1890), a Dade County attorney before the war, active as an area recruiter, commanded a third of Shelby's force on the Marshall raid.

3. Shanghai, a settlement in NE31, Drywood Township, 3½ miles west of present Sheldon, Mo. A Confederate hotbed, it was devastated in the war and did not survive it.

The pursuit continued to Neosho, Newtonia, and Granby, Mo.

Thursday, October 29. We was up before day and fed our horses and eat a scanty ration, and at daylight our command was again moving forward and rain commenced falling. Col. Weer took a few men and pushed on to the Fort as no whisky could be had short of that place and his supply was exhausted. Col. Clark took command. Before reaching Big Drywood Creek the rain came down heavy and continued until night. We passed Genl Blunts Train at Dry Wood enroute to Fort Smith, Ark. We arrived at the Fort near sunset and camped in dwellings and such shelter as we was able to find, a terible sleet was falling and we was wet to our bodies and very cold. Whiskey was drank freely by the troops and a pandemonium soon began in which one soldier shot another accidentally but not killing him. We marched about 30 miles today.

Friday, October 30. I was up till midnight. I looked for a quiet place to sleep last night but that place could not be found in Fort Scott where seven or eight hundred men in federal uniforms and under the influence of Evil Spirits had possession of the place and all places where moist damnation was kept. And the night was one hell or pandemonium, as some of the oldest inhabitants said this morning, the like was never experienced here before and it seemed that hell had established Head Quarters at Fort Scott. I laid down to sleep in the Bar room of the Fort Scott House, but soon a number of soldiers found their way here and commenced a Love feast. I found that sleep was a luxury not obtainable. So I joined the Love feast. This morning I took my men and returned to Balltown. The ground was froze and day very cold, arrived at camp this afternoon at 2 O'clock. *(Porter's entries Oct. 31 through Nov. 4 concerned only routine matters.)*

Thursday, November 5. I spent the day in Camp but found nothing exciting. The guerrillas have not disturbed our locality of late, so our commands are now inactive. Many of the families in our locality have moved away or came near our camp lately, so the guerrillas can't find subsistence. Today pleasant. *(Nov. 6-8 are omitted.)*

Monday, November 9. I find myself in the best of health and would like to keep so, but fear too great amount of inactivity may engender disease. We have some few sick in camp, one of my Company by name of Johnson is very low with Typhoid fever. I have nothing to mention of this day very interesting. Day pleasant.

Tuesday, November 10. This morning at 3 O'clock 15 minutes, John H. Johnson proper name Davis[1] died of Typhoid fever. He was a member of my Company. The name of Johnson he assumed when he enlisted as he ran away from home, and took this precaution that his parents might not find him. I was engaged making his coffin today. Day cool and pleasant.

1. Private Hiram C. (Hiram M. in the Roster) Davis, brother of Simeon Bennett Davis (see note Sept. 23). In September 1992, on the evidence of Porter's journal, Herb and Gordon C. Davis, Denver, grandsons of Simeon and great-nephews of Hiram Davis, obtained a new government veteran's marker for the grave, bearing the proper name, and a full-dress Civil War-era military funeral was reenacted.

Wednesday, November 11. Lieut. Willsey went up to Fort Scott this morning on business connected with our companies. At 10 O'clock this morning the funeral escort took up its line of march with the remains of the soldier Johnson to the little Cemetery near Balltown where we laid him away to rest in due military honors. He had one brother in our company to mourn his loss, and his comrades express great sorrow in the loss of their companion in arms. The day was very windy, afternoon I spent a few hours at Mr. Austins.

Thursday, November 12. I spent the day in camp. Lieut. Willsey returned from the Fort this afternoon. About dark Parson Durans[1] and J. I. Moore[2] came in camp from Nevada, and reported 5 Robbers in their vicinity who were robbing the citizens of money and other articles of value. I took 10 men of Cos. "A" and "F" and started in pursuit. On my arrival in the neighborhood of Nevada I learned from the citizens that many had been robbed, and the villains had returned in the direction of Fort Scott an hour before we arrived. They was supposed to be Kansas men. I pursued them 5 miles west of Nevada and finding our game had made good their escape, the Parson who accompanied us invited us to stop at his house near by until morning as it was now midnight, we done so and was comfortably provided during our stay. The day and night pleasant.

1. Unidentified. A William C. Duren (1837-1912) and family members are buried in Deepwood Cemetery in Nevada. Mannen Duren, 35, born in Missouri, and family appear in the 1870 census for Center Township.

2. Several J. Moores are listed in the 1860 census; this may be Joseph Moore, 46, a farmer in Center Township.

Friday, November 13. This morning early Parson Durans very estimable lady prepared a good breakfast for a portion of my mess while the remainder went over to a widow Samples[1] near by and procured breakfast. After breakfast we discovered two men approaching us in the distance, when we prepared to capture them, the men at Mrs. Samples fell in behind them and I came up in front, when the two men turned and fled with all speed and a lively race soon brought them to a stop when we found them loyal citizens, one was named Thomas Puckett[2] an old man. I turned them loose and went east ten miles, found all quiet. Returned to camp at sunset. *(Nov. 14-15 are omitted.)*

1. "Colonel" Smiley H. Sample, who in 1857 settled in NE9 Deerfield Township, was shot through the heart by Kansas Redlegs in March, 1862, at age 58.

2. Thomas Puckett, 48, blacksmith, of Center Township.

Monday, November 16. I spent the day in camp, and by frequent observation I was able to discover some life in our camp. Oscar Nelson[1] a member of Post Battery of Fort Scott and Mr. Ehle[2] of Wis. and Mr. Louis Willson[3] a citizen with Lieut Willsey and some of our boys went out to hunt deer this afternoon, but had no success. We had a heavy frost last night. Day pleasant. *(Nov. 17-27 are omitted.)*

1. Of a prominent Little Osage pioneer family, Oscar M. Nelson must have changed sides. In October 1861 he was 3rd Lt. in the 7th Cavalry of the 8th Division, Missouri State Guard (Confederate). After the war he was Vernon County sheriff and a prominent Nevadan, unlikely for a dedicated Federal.

2. Marshall M. Ehle, Oconto, Wis., Adjutant of the 2nd Battalion of the Regiment.

3. Possibly J. L. Wilson, 38, a farmer in Osage Township.

Saturday, November 28. I spent the evening with the lady friends on the hill last evening, and presume I shall in the future be deprived of their good company as our Co. will move tomorrow twelve miles away. This morning I went in company with Captains Vittum and Carpenter and a few of our boys to Fort

Scott to be paid. We had a very cold ride and I froze my right ear very bad. We was all paid up to October 31st 1863. We did not receive our pay until this afternoon. Major Bowen U.S.A. Paymaster. We remained in Fort Scott tonight, stopped at the Wilder House.[1] Day very cold. I learn that my Co. moved to the Douglas place on Marmaton River at the mouth of Big Dry Wood today.[2]

1. At the corner of Main and Wall streets. Louis Wilder was an early settler of Center Township in Vernon County.—*The History of Vernon County, Mo.*, 585.

2. NE6 Deerfield Township, settled in 1834 by Colonel George Douglass (sic), whose large log house was known as "the Log Castle." The property passed to his son-in-law Captain Henry Clay Cogswell, in 1863 absent in the Confederate army. The site overlooked the major ford over the Marmaton River.

Sunday, November 29. I remained in Fort Scott this afternoon and had a good time with other officers of my Regiment. Afternoon I rode out to our new camp in company with Capt. Vittum, John White a scout and Private Wm Stoner[1] of my Company. We found the Company comfortably located, Captain Carpenter and Co. "A" remain at Balltown. Our camp is located 12 miles east of Fort Scott. . . .

1. Private William H. Stoner, Baraboo, Wis.

Monday, November 30. I commenced the work of today by first erecting a bunk or place to sleep upon in our room occupied as our Head Quarters and

Officers room in the old Cogswell or Douglas building as it was called. All hands was busy making their quarters comfortable for the winter and providing comfortable stables for our horses, as the weather is beginning to increase in severity. I commenced work again this afternoon on our co. Returns with Capt. Vittums bid in drawing up the papers properly I became expert in the business and feel confident that when we accomplish the Returns in full I will be able to conduct the business alone while the Captain is absent. Our camp has presented an active and busy look today. Tonight we are sitting by a good fire in the fireplace in our room, and old black Joe our servant nodding in the corner. Day pleasant. *(Dec 1-5 are omitted.)*

Sunday, December 6. This morning Lieut Willsey and Privates Wm Stoner and H. M. Russell[1] of my Company started to their homes in Wisconsin on Furlough and leave the of absence the former [sic]. I bought a fine dapple gray horse this morning of Edwin Requa[2] a citizen; paid $80.00 for him. I was ordered to Balltown this morning to transact some army business with Capt. Carpenter for Capt. Vittum. My brother W. D. Porter and a citizen by name of Louis Requa[3] accompanied me. We visited the ladies at Mr. Austins this evening and found them as interesting as usual. Mr. Requa was a cousin to the young ladies we visited. We had a good visit. . . . *(Dec. 7-8 are omitted.)*

1. Private Horace M. Russell, Baraboo, Wis.
2. Edward Requa, 25, farmer.

3. Lewis C. Requa, 22, brother of above; both sons of James Harvey Requa, prominent farmer and early settler; locally pronounced *REE-quay.*

Wednesday, December 9. This morning I was ordered to take command of a detachment of my Company and go by way of Balltown and take as many more of Co. "A" and proceed to Papinsville and kill and dress a number of hogs for our use, that were roaming at large. On my arrival at Balltown, Capt. Carpenter informed me that it would be impossible to furnish the men today and requested me to stop until morning and my demand could be complied with. I done as requested. The day was very cloudy.

Thursday, December 10. This morning I was joined by a portion of Co. "A" when I took up my journey to Papinsville when we arrived at 1 O'clock P.M. and camped at Mrs. Barrows[1] east of town, where I found a good house to stop in and a large barn for our horses, as the place was deserted. . . .

1. Freeman Barrows, a pioneer settler, schoolteacher, public official, and merchant, died at the beginning of the war. The house referred to (still standing, one of the few in Bates County to survive the war) is in NE23 Prairie Township. According to Robert S. Barrows, Rochester, N.Y., a descendant, after Order No. 11 Asenath Barrows and her five daughters went to Osceola, Mo., probably in October, 1863, and returned in the spring of 1865. The three teenaged sons, Theodore, Freeman, and William, stayed in the neighborhood and "must have gotten some rations for rendering small services" to the occupation authorities. The family was "Old Whig"—anti-slavery.

Friday, December 11. This morning we got everything ready to scald and dress the hogs we are to kill. I sent out some of the men in search of hogs and they soon found and killed nine very large ones which was all nicely dressed before night. A messenger came to us from camp with orders not to kill any more hogs as it was feared the meat would spoil, the weather not being cold enough. The messenger stated that the portion of my Company that had been on duty at Humboldt, Kans.[1] had came back to our Camp before he left. Day very cloudy.

1. In southwest Allen County, Kan., south of Iola, visited by Missourians on September 7, and again on October 14, 1861. The latter visit "left the town in ashes." "Lane's men claimed that they burned Osceola because the rebel raiders had robbed and plundered Humboldt. Col. Talbot's men claimed they burned Humboldt in retaliation for the burning of Osceola."—*History of Vernon County,* 290.

Saturday, December 12. This morning we started back to our companies, arrived at Balltown at 1 O'clock P.M. I had some business to transact with Capt. Carpenter which detained me this afternoon, so I sent my Co. Boys on to our camp, which is named Camp Insley.[1] The day has been very rainy. Capt. Carpenter and myself spent the evening at Mr. Austins.

1. Named for Captain Merritt H. Insley, quartermaster of U.S. Volunteers at Fort Scott.

Sunday, December 13. This morning I started

to Camp Insley. Capt. Carpenter, Wm. H. Hewelt[1] our Regth Adjutant and Bro. Walworth[2] accompanied me. After a ride of 12 miles we arrived at Camp in time. The day was cloudy and cold.

1. William H. Hewitt, Kingston, Wis., was regimental adjutant.

2. The diarist's brother, Walworth D. Porter.

Monday, December 14. This morning Capts. Vittum, Carpenter and Lieut. Hewett went to Co. "D" of our Regiment on Dry Wood[1] 4 miles distant from our camp. Capt. Vittum returned to camp this evening. I spent the day in camp and was idle. Some of the boys was out after forage. The day was very cold, but Old Joe keeps up a good fire for me. *(Dec. 15-17 are omitted.)*

1. At Lambert Ford, NE25 Deerfield Township, on Big Drywood Creek, 3½ miles south of present Deerfield, Mo.

Friday, December 18. I took twelve men of my Company and went out on a reconnoiter in the neighborhood of Nevada and beyond to the Mounds[1] 15 miles east of camp. We took dinner at Uncle Billy Ellises north of Nevada. We scouted over the country near the Mounds and put up for the night at a widow Clintons[2] near the Mounds. We suffered terribly with the extreme cold of today and found no face of the enemy in our journey. We saw many deer and wild turkeys today. *(Dec. 19-22 are omitted.)*

1. Properly the Dodson Mounds, after pioneer settler Dr. J. L. D. Dodson, but also called Walker Hill or Prewitt Hill, after W. H. Prewitt; located roughly in Sections 8 and 9, Walker Township. A series of other eminences, Howard's Mound (including the highest point in Vernon County), Hamlin's Mound, and the Blue Mounds, extend several miles north-northeastwards.

2. Probably the widow of pioneer settler Maj. Bennett J. Clinton, who in 1860 was 48 and a farmer in Center Township.

Wednesday, December 23. I remained in camp this forenoon. This afternoon I rode out two miles west of camp to Pitmans Mill[1] to engage a carpenter to make me a Camp Chest. But he was unable to do the work as he was sick. The day has been quite pleasant and a little thaw took place.

1. James H. Pitman, 38, was a farmer in Deerfield Township.

Thursday, December 24. I was in camp all day. The boys was getting up a dance party to day to take place at the residence of Notingham[1] near Pitman Mills. I attended the dance or country hoe-down where both Soldier and citizen drank freely of a very peculiar liquid they called Whiskey. I inspected sample and thought there was a mistake in the name. I am of the opinion that if the compound had been resolved into its first principles there might have been found Bedbug juice, Jimpson burs, rotten Tobacco, Nitric Acid, and all the calamities that befall the human family. I remained until a late hour when the performance closed. I then returned to camp with my brain weighted down with brilliant ideas. The day was warm and pleasant.

1. W. J. Notingham, 53, a carpenter; in 1860 he was residing in the home of William C. Welch in Henry Township.

Friday, December 25. We received word from the Fort that Quantrells troop was expected to attack us. Capt. Vittum sent me to Balltown to notify Carpenter, J. Doppler accompanied me. I took dinner at Mr. Austins with Capt. Carpenter and with him spent the afternoon there very agreeably with the ladies. I attended a dance in the Camp tonight. Today cloudy. Rain this evening. *(Dec. 26-31 are omitted.)*

1864

Friday, January 1. I remained in camp today and was writing on my Company papers. The day has been extremely cold. There was a dance three miles from camp and some of my Company attended tonight.

Saturday, January 2. This morning before day the boys who attended the dance returned with fingers, toes, and ears froze, and some profanity and groaning was indulged in as soon as they came to the fire. I spent the day in writing up my Company papers. Capt. Vittum and Orderly Sergt. Cooper went to Fort Scott this afternoon, quiet reigns supreme in our camp at this time. The health of the Company is good. The day has been very cold.

Sunday, January 3. I remained in camp this forenoon and was idle. I received an invitation from Mrs. Sample and daughter to take dinner with them this afternoon. At noon I was prepared to go. John White our Scout, J. M. Smith,[1] M. Kivell,[2] and C. S. Foster[3] of my Company went with me. After a ride of two miles in a south east course we arrived at the place. The widow and daughter received us in a lady like manner, and dinner was served in due time, which was got up in the best style of culinary art. A fine Roast Turkey was set before me to carve. I took up the carving instruments, and soon performed the duty in a scientific manner. Well, we had one of the best dinners, after which the widow a gay and fascinating lady, and her daughter Dosha[4] entertained us in a pleasant manner, until near night, when we took leave of our hostess, and returned to camp. The day very cold. *(Jan. 4-5 are omitted.)*

1. Private Joseph M. Smith, Oshkosh, Wis.; deserted Sept. 20, 1864.
2. Private Bart Kivell, Springfield, Wis.
3. Private Charles S. Foster, Baraboo, Wis.
4. Dosha, or Dosia, Sample is not enumerated in the 1860 census.

Wednesday, January 6. Capt. Carpenter who has been appointed to visit our Companies and enlist men for Veterans[1] was at our Camp today, and succeeded in enlisting the following members of my Company for the Veteran Corps. John F. Greening, Daniel Williams,[2] J. M. Smith, Chas. H. Pratt,[3] Michael Kivell,[4] Wm. C. Wright,[5] Wm. Mitchell,[6] and Alexander Preston.[7] The Captain then went to Co. "D" and Co. "C" of our Regiment who are camped on Dry Wood 4 and 7 miles from us,[8] where he expects to procure more Veterans. There was nothing more to disturb our quiet today. The day was very cold. *(Jan. 7-13 are omitted.)*

1. The three-year enlistments of 1861 were expiring. The army mounted a campaign to induce men to reenlist for three more years or the duration of the war. Those who did so were accorded the title "Veteran Volunteers" and given bonuses and furloughs.
2. Private Daniel Williams, Madison, Wis.
3. Private Charles H. Pratt, Baraboo, Wis.
4. Private Michael Keivell, Winfield, Wis.
5. Private William C. Wright, Ironton, Wis.

6. Private William Mitchell, Baraboo, Wis.
7. Private Alexander Preston, Appleton, Wis.
8. Company C was stationed on the West Fork of Big Drywood Creek, two miles south of present Garland, Kansas.

Thursday, January 14. This morning Capt. Vittum with a detail of fifteen men of our Company started on a Scout in Cedar Co., Mo. The Captain turned the command of Company over to me while he was absent. I have adopted a drill service to take place daily, both mounted and on foot which relieves a great deal of monotony. Today more moderate in temperature. *(Jan. 15-17 are omitted.)*

Monday, January 18. The day dawned upon us very pleasant. After the duties of the morning had been disposed of the boys brought out all surplus clothing and their blankets and aired them and commenced cleaning quarters and camp generally, dirt and rubbish was hurried out of camp limits and soon our temporary abodes presented a more cheerful look of comfort and health. Today cool, but pleasant. There was a dance at Nevada tonight at Dr. Rules,[1] some of my Company attended.

1. Dr. P. G. Rule, 35, wife Francis, 40, both born in Kentucky. An infant son of theirs is buried at Deerfield.

Tuesday, January 19. Capt. Vittum and his detachment returned from scout today. They report having a lively fight with about 40 guerrillas at Horse Creek, Cedar County. The result of the engagement was 7 of the enemy was killed and 11 horses and Equipments was captured. One horse of our Company was wounded slightly. Our men escaped injury. Those of the enemy who escaped took a north course, and our boys pursued them some distance without any satisfactory results. . . . *(Jan. 20-23 are omitted.)*

Sunday, January 24. Capt. Vittum started to Kansas City on business connected with the army. I went to Balltown this morning to confer with Capt. Carpenter in relation to our opening the spring campaign. After making our arrangements satisfactory, we went to Mr. Austins where we had a pleasant visit with the family, and the young ladies especially, made our stay very interesting. I returned to my Company this evening and Ethan Wyman[1] also who accompanied me. Today mild and pleasant. *(Jan. 25-26 are omitted.)*

1. Private Ethan Wyman, Baraboo, Wis.

Wednesday, January 27. We are looking forward in anxious expectation to the reappearance of the Devils Knightenants, as the pleasant weather we may have will undoubtedly bring them from their lairs. I have not been very busy today. I was entertained by some fine Violin Music today, which was finely executed by some members of my Company. Today very pleasant. *(Jan. 28-Feb. 1 are omitted.)*

Tuesday, February 2. I received a dispatch from Fort Scott ordering a detachment of 40 men and a Sergeant to accompany Major Genl. Saml. Curtis as Escort to Fort Smith, Ark. the distance being 180 miles from Fort Scott. The troops that were detailed to go was busy making the necessary preparations to start tomorrow morning. This evening the Detachment from my Company in command of Sergt. Eli M. Cooper left camp to join the remaining portion of Escort 6 miles distant on the road. There was nothing farther of mention with us today. Today warm and pleasant. *(Feb. 3-6 are omitted.)*

Sunday, February 7. We had a quiet day in camp. Some citizens came to visit us, and gratify their morbid curiosity, while others came to sell Butter, Eggs and other articles not usual in a Soldiers ration. Our boys use a little economy and save coffee and sugar out of their rations which they exchange for such as Butter, Eggs, Potatoes and Chickens. There is no report of guerrillas in our neighborhood yet. Day cool.

Monday, February 8. Lieut. Willsey returned from Wisconsin today in company of a large number of Recruits for our Regiments of which 31 joined our Company today. I went to Fort Scott on business connected with my Co. and returned this evening. Day pleasant. *(Feb. 9 is omitted.)*

Wednesday, February 10. This day I celebrate my 32nd year, but I have no extra Bill of Fare to partake of as is customary on birthday occasions. I took down my battered Canteen and found a quart of extra corn juice which had been distilled, and a portion soon changed its locality. I spent a portion of the day with some of the new Recruits who lately came from my home place, and they gave me an interesting account of home and former acquaintances. Outside of my daily duties I have been idle. All have been quiet and enjoying themselves as well as our surroundings will admit of. Today some cool. *(Feb. 11 is omitted.)*

Friday, February 12. Having some military business to transact with Capt. Carpenter I rode over to Balltown to see him this forenoon. I found all of his company quite well and anxious for the spring campaign to open. I had a pleasant time with the whole souled Captain and our business was soon transpired. The boys was preparing for a dance tonight, and I was urged to remain and take part in their entertainment. After a good Camp dinner the Captain and myself visited the ladies on the hill, where happiness reigns supreme. Well we had a lovely visit and a good supper. We returned to camp in time to take part in the opening set of the evening. There was many ladies present who can not be surpassed in the country for beauty and elegance of manners. As I have set in for the night I will make an end of my days account by saying it was quite cool. *(Feb. 13 is omitted.)*

Sunday, February 14. We had Company Inspection this morning, after which the boys resume their customary habits. Those who usually serve the Devil, played Cards and Ball, while those of a Godly nature, read their Bibles and sang Hymns. I judge the God serving portion of my Company as small, if we take profanity as a standard in summing up our conclusions. Today very pleasant.

Monday, February 15. I learn that Capt. Vittum returned to Fort Scott last evening from Kansas City. Our Battalion HeadQuarters was established in Camp Insley, our Camp, our Captain Vittum was appointed Commander of Balltown and Lieut. C. W. Porter Battalion Adjutant. I have not been very busy today. Today very pleasant. *(Feb. 16-17 are omitted.)*

Thursday, February 18. General Curtis arrived in Fort Scott today, and our company boys who escorted the Genl. to Fort Smith, Ark. arrived in camp in a very depressed and tumultuous manner, declaring they would take the life of our Commissary Sergeant, Morris E. Waite who they claimed sold the ten days rations that was drawn for them to subsist on while gone as Escort, causing them to make the trip of 180 miles with empty stomachs. Waite did not wait, but made his escape to Fort Scott as a city of refuge, where he had better stay, if he values his life, for a lead mine would soon be located about his person if he returns to the Company. No other excitement with us today. Today very cold. *(Feb. 19-20 are omitted.)*

Sunday, February 21. Capt. Vittum arrived in camp this forenoon from the Fort. This afternoon the Capt. and myself called together those of the Company who Escorted Genl. Curtis to Fort Smith and we thoroughly investigated the ration question which caused the late commotion between the company and Sergt. Waite. We find from the evidence that Waite drew 10 days Rations for 40 men and sold all but enough for supper and breakfast and appropriated the money to his own use, thus the men were obliged to go five days without food and march 180 miles. There was nothing else worthy of note took place with us today. Today some cold. *(Feb. 22 is omitted.)*

Tuesday, February 23. I had considerable business to transact with the Ordnance and Quarter Master Departments today, which occupied my time until evening. I then started to Camp alone and had with me a large amount of money belong [sic] to my Company. When I had gone four miles on my road, I discovered two suspicious characters standing in the road in a dense woods and just in front of me. I rode up to them with my revolver in hand when they separated on either side of the road, my suspicions was confirmed as to their intentions. I leveled my revolver upon them and ordered them to mount their horses and go on a gallop toward Fort Scott and if they looked back I should not be responsible if they turned into a pillar of salt, but would try and make places of ventilation about their persons. After they departed I rode on to camp without farther molestation. Today very pleasant but some windy. *(Feb. 22-26 are omitted.)*

Saturday, February 27. I finished my Returns

this forenoon. Afternoon I resumed work on my Pay Rolls. I learn that guerrillas was seen ten miles east of our camp last evening. I shall hunt them tomorrow, and disturb their quiet if I strike their locality. . . .

Sunday, February 28. I took 20 men this morning and started on a scout. I passed through Nevada and then took a north east course three miles and on entering some timber I discovered a camp of 30 Bushwhackers. I distributed my men, and charged the camp before the enemy was aware we was near. As we approached the camp a few shots was fired by the enemy, wounding one horse of my Company. The boys fired in rapid succession killing five of the enemy and one horse, the wounded if any escaped. The enemy left their camp and provisions with us. We destroyed their provisions, and brought away 11 horses and 19 saddles, 7 Double barrel guns, 6 good Revolvers and some quilts and blankets, as trophies of our victory. The enemy escaped in various directions, thinking without a doubt that total annihilation was their doom if they remained to fight. We camped on Marmaton river fifteen miles from Company. Day pleasant.

Monday, February 29. I found the enemy had assembled and had gone in a north course. After we partook of our scanty breakfast we started in pursuit and after a rapid march of 12 miles we met a scouting party of Co. "A" in command of Lieut. Ellis who informed that that they had a skirmish with the Bushwhackers this morning and killed two men and captured one horse, and the enemy fled in confusion. I gave up farther pursuit and returned to camp, where I arrived at 4 O'clock P.M. and found all quiet. Today very cold. *(Mar. 1-6 are omitted.)*

Monday, March 7. I finished my Pay Rolls today, which is quite a relief to me. I am informed that Capt. Vittum has been detailed to serve on Court Martial at Fort Scott today, as there has been a large number of soldiers and citizens placed in the Guard House who have committed offence against military law, and it becomes necessary to try their cases. Today has been tolerable pleasant and not very windy. *(Mar. 8-9 are omitted.)*

Thursday, March 10. We are informed that Doctor Leonard Dodge our Physician while at Balltown died this morning of Pleurisy at his home on Little Osage near Balltown. The community have lost a good man and our troops feel the loss of their benefactor who so faithfully administered to them when sick and wounded and to those of our comrades in their dying moments. All has been quiet with us today. . . .

Friday, March 11. This morning Brother Walworth and myself rode to Balltown to attend the funeral of Dr. Dodge. Capt. Carpenter took charge of a portion of his Company and I joined him when we marched to the Doctors Residence where a large assemblage of citizens had arrived. The time appointed for the occasion 11 O'clock A.M. having arrived, the daughter of the Dr. played a dirge upon the organ, after which Revd Baldwin[1] offered an appropriate prayer, and the Procession was formed by military & citizens and so arranged as to listen to a sermon delivered by our Chaplain, Baldwin, the Text was Pauls Epistle to the Romans 1st Chapter 10th verse, after which the remains were conveyed to the cemetery at Balltown and laid in their final resting place. After the funeral was conducted myself and Brother W was invited to dinner at Mr. Austins after which the family entertained us very agreeably a few hours when we went to the camp of Co. "A" and stayed until morning. This forenoon cold and cloudy, afternoon was pleasant.

1. John S. Baldwin, Mukwonago, Wis., regimental chaplain.

Saturday, March 12. At 2 O'clock this morning myself and brother started to our Company, arrived in camp before day. Capt. Vittum came to Company from Fort Scott today. John Dennis[1] returned to Co. from Desertion June 10, 1862, having so returned by Order of Courtmartial. Our Commissary Sergt. M. E. Waite was discharged from the service today, thus escaping the wrath of the Co. for stealing rations, and compelling them to go 180 miles without food. . . .

1. Private John Dennis, Baraboo, Wis.

Sunday, March 13. I was busy assisting Capt. Vittum in fixing up some Company and Battalion matters that required immediate attention. We succeeded in accomplishing all we set out to do before night when the Capt. expressed himself satisfied and we then took a walk over to Judge Harvey Requas where we took supper and spent a few hours very pleasant and returned to camp. . . . *(Mar. 14-16 are omitted.)*

Thursday, March 17. I was attending to making up my Company papers today. At 4 O'clock P.M. I accompanied our Regtl Surgeon Wm. H. Warner[1] in an ambulance to Co. "A" at Balltown on business. When we got there we found the Company prepared for a dance and bringing in the neighborhood ladies to enjoy their festivities. We was cordially invited to join them which we did. The day was moderate, but some cloudy. *(Mar. 18-23 are omitted.)*

1. William H. Warner, Oconomowoc, Wis., First Assistant Surgeon of the Regiment.

Thursday, March 24. I was busy this forenoon writing up my Company papers. Afternoon I took my Company out on Drill, after which I rode out two miles to Isaac Evans[1] to visit his daughter Mrs. Rowntree[2] a widow. I spent an hour very agreeable with her and her two sisters. I could not remain long with them a shower was approaching so I hastened to camp. At 4 O'clock P.M. the storm came and was continuing at the time I retired for the night. . . . *(Mar. 25 is omitted.)*

1. Unidentified, but see note Nov. 28, 1864.

2. The only Roundtree (sic) in the 1860 census was J. P. Roundtree, 35, farmer in Drywood Township; wife M. J., 18; both born in Missouri. According to report John Roundtree, the first person to be buried in Moore Cemetery south of Nevada, was a Negro slave of James H. Moore.

Saturday, March 26. Capt. Vittum came from the Fort this morning and we spent the day in attending to business that belonged to our Battalion which required a great amount of writing. This evening the Capt. and myself was called upon to lay out our near neighbor Mr. Orr[1] who had just died of Ersipelas. Today very pleasant.

1. William C. Orr, 45, farmer in Deerfield Township, born in Tennessee; wife M. H., 22, born in Arkansas.

Sunday, March 27. I remained in camp not very busy until 4 O'clock this evening when I attended the funeral of Mr. Orr. A small number of my Company attended and many citizens. The day was very windy. *(Mar. 28 is omitted.)*

Tuesday, March 29. We learn this morning that notorious Bushwhacker Pony Hill and command had again arrived in our neighborhood. So I took 20 men and went in hunt of him, and five miles east of Nevada I discovered 4 men of guerrillas stripe when we gave them a lively run for a half mile keeping up a lively fire upon them when one of their horses and rider fell dead and was knocked off his horse by a limb and with revolver in each hand fought us until fifteen shots had took effect, ending the life worthy a better cause than the one he was engaged in. After securing his horse we returned to camp. Day cold & rainy.

Wednesday, March 30. I went to Fort Scott this morning and attended to some necessary business and returned this evening. I learn that Capt. Carpenter succeed last night with his men in surprising Pony Hills camp and capturing all but the men who escaped. Six horses and some guns was captured. Today pleasant. *(Mar. 31-Apr. 2 are omitted.)*

Sunday, April 3. I had Company inspection this morning and found Arms, Equipments, and Camp in good condition. After inspection a number of the Co. went to church at the Modrell School House[1] about 1½ miles from camp. Afternoon a heavy shower visited us with heavy thunder and a great amount of lightning.

1. Named for pioneer settler William Modrel, then a 59-year-old farmer. His home (in which General Sterling Price would spend a night that fall) and the schoolhouse lay just west-southwest of modern Deerfield, Mo.

Monday, April 4. This morning I took command of 20 men of my Co. and started on a reconnoiter about fifteen miles east of camp to see if any of the enemy were there. About 6 miles from camp I learned that 30 guerrillas were secreted in the woods and would likely give us a hard fight. I soon found their locality and made an immediate attack, I had my men in a secure position when we opened a brisk fire upon the enemy for 15 or 20 minutes and they in return gave us a lively round and as soon as they began to weaken I charged their position and they made a lively retreat. We captured 9 horses and some guns, killed 5 men and 2 horses. We had one horse wounded, no other loss. We found it unnecessary to go farther so returned to camp. Day some stormy.

Tuesday, April 5. . . . I rode out to visit the widow Redfield[1] and Mrs. Rowntree at which places I had a pleasant visit. *(Apr. 6-11 are omitted.)*

1. Pioneer settler Abram, or Abraham, Redfield had died December 8, 1862. His widow, Phoebe or Feba, would have been 68 years old. "She was probably 'the widow Redfield,' unless one of David's older brothers, John (born ca. 1838) or William (born ca. 1840), had died leaving a *young* widow."—Shirley Harris Park, Tulsa, Okla. Redfield was the founder of Deerfield, Mo., and would have been its namesake save for his own objections. Reportedly, just at the moment, a deer bounded through the settlement, and the proposed name was altered in commemoration. His son David, however, managed to attach the family name to Redfield, Kansas, 30 miles due west.

Tuesday, April 12. This morning early I took command of my Company (leaving sufficient to guard camp) and went to Fort Scott to be paid off. Was paid by Major J. Bowen U.S. Pay Master to include the 29th of February 1864, was paid this forenoon. Afternoon was like all pay days one given to a drunken carouse. My negro waiter (Joe) had a desperate combat with another negro in the Fort who was said to be their bully, but Joe gave him a terrible thrashing and some of the boy beat the negroes head in a shocking manner, with clubs and was prevented from killing him by the Commander of the Fort. Joe received a bad cut on the head by the negro in the fight. I returned to camp in Company with Capt. Carpenter and Lieut. Willsey this evening. Today very pleasant.

Wednesday, April 13. I remained in camp today. Many of the boys are out procuring partners for a dance at Mr. Pitmans tonight, and two miles west of camp I secured Mrs. Rowntree as my partner and attended the festivities of the evening, and at midnight as I close the events of today the dance is progressing. Geo. Knight[1] returned from furlough today. Day pleasant. *(Apr. 14-15 are omitted.)*

1. Private George C. Knight, Roxbury, Wis.

Saturday, April 16. . . . Afternoon Hiram Statia of my Co. who had been paying his devotions to Mrs. Rowntree asked me to accompany him to the ladies residence and make her and sisters a visit, so we rode out there where we had a fine visit, though Statia told me that Mrs. R. had cooled his affection for her, and that I had brought the result to a terminus while he was absent at Fort Gibson. But I declared myself innocent of the charge and I satisfied him that I had not interfered. We returned to camp in due time. . . .

Sunday, April 17. Some rainy this morning but cleared away by 10 O'clock A.M. and I went to Judge Harvey Requas by invitation to take of a wedding dinner provided on the occasion of his son Edwards marriage to Miss Mollie Rule[1] daughter of Dr. Rule of Nevada, Mo. I had a grand time while there with Misses Florence Requa[2] and Mollie Daugherty.[3] I returned to camp in due time after partaking of an exceeding fine dinner seldom excelled on like occasions. Afternoon very pleasant.

1. Not in the 1860 census. For Dr. Rule, see Note 1, January 18, 1864.

2. Florence Requa, 18, daughter of James Harvey and Mary A. Requa.

3. A familiar surname in the neighborhood in more recent times. In the 1850 census John Dougherty (sic), 30, born in Ireland, was enumerated with his family; in 1870 his son Hugh Dorherty (sic), 48, born in Ireland, resided with his family in Richland Township; but no mention of Mollie.

Monday, April 18. . . . The coast being clear I concluded to visit Mrs. Rowntree this evening. H. J. Case[1] of my Co. accompanied me to see Miss Alice, Mrs. Rs sister. We had a splendid visit, and I found Mrs. R had discharged H. S. and I have presented myself as a victim to womans caprice. Day pleasant. *(Apr. 19-23 are omitted.)*

1. Private Harrison J. Case, Baraboo, Wis.

Sunday, April 24. This morning at 9 O'clock

John H. McPherson[1] of my Company and Miss Angie Evans[2] were united in marriage by Parson Hogan[3] at the residence of the Brides father Isaac Evans. I was not present at the wedding, but was on time to take my place at the table so bountifully supplied with eatables of which I done justice too. After dinner I was engaged in pleasant conversation with Mrs. Rowntree until late in the evening. On my return to Camp I found Lieut. Willsey had arrived from the Fort and had arrested H. A. Brooks of my Co. for drunkenness and disorderly conduct, when he became so abusive that the Lieut. tied him to a limb of a tree by the thumbs and put a gag in his mouth to stop his vile abuse. Today has been cloudy and some rain. *(Apr. 25-26 are omitted.)*

1. Private John H. McPherson, Baraboo, Wis.
2. Unidentified, but see note Nov. 28, 1864.
3. Rev. David H. Hogan, a pioneer settler, resided near "Hogan's Ford" about three miles south of Deerfield (SE Section 13); this was the central point of the September 1861 skirmish known as the Battle of Drywood.

Wednesday, April 27. This morning I sent out a scouting party of 20 men in command of Sergeant Luce to Clear Creek and Capt. Vittum went to Fort Scott. We had a hearty rain today accompanied with thunder and lightning. The river Marmaton by us is rising very rapidly this evening. . . .

Thursday, **April 28.** . . . Afternoon I changed my occupation by saddling Old Dick and riding out to visit Mrs. R. where I remained until dusk of evening gave warning that I must take my departure. I had a very agreeable visit. Today cloudy and has the appearance of more rain soon.

Friday, April 29. . . . The boys return from the Scout wet and hungry, they did not discover any enemy, but reported that the citizens at Clear Creek told them that a large force of Bushwhackers or guerrillas numbering 70 men had gone northward the day before our Scouts arrived. The boys would likely had a warm time if they had met the 70 guerrillas as my men numbered 20 men, but Sergt. Luce in command would have shown himself equal to do all that would have been required of him, and that is whip the cowardly, thieving devils. . . .

Saturday, April 30. . . . E. N. Marsh a citizen of Baraboo Wis. and comrade in the 1st Wis. Infantry Regt. came to visit us today, and this evening was spent in bringing to light our early experience in soldier and camp life in 1861. At dark a man by name of Carpenter[1] and a fellow companion came in camp, he proved to be a scout and Detective in the government employ. He gave us an interesting account of his capture and escape from Quantrells guerrillas. Forenoon cloudy. Afternoon pleasant.

1. Unidentified. Oliver H. Carpenter, Montello, Wis., was a sergeant in Company C, but it seems likely Porter would have so identified him, if this were he.

Sunday, May 1. This morning the two Detectives left us and went their way. I had Company Inspection at 10 O'clock A.M. after which I was unemployed the rest of the day. At sunset I rode out to spend the evening with Mrs. R. and Private H. J. Case went with me to tell Miss Alice Evans how dearly he loved her. Well, I will not tell what was said, but we had a very interesting visit and returned to camp at 9 O'clock P.M. *(May 2-4 are omitted.)*

Thursday, May 5. I put up at the Wilder House last night and was very busy attending to my business a part of the day. I learn that Major Henning of 2nd Bat. 3rd Wis. Cav. was united in marriage to a young lady of Fort Scott this morning. The day has been very windy. I returned to camp this evening and called on Mrs. Rowntree on my way and took supper with her and sisters, and then went to camp.

Friday, May 6. . . . I sent Bro. W. D. Porter in command of 20 men of Co. on a scout at Pleasant run 10 miles from camp where I learn guerrillas are congregating. The day has been pleasant.

Saturday, May 7. . . . Sergt. W. D. Porter and command returned from Scout this afternoon and report that 18 guerrillas had been on Pleasant Run two days before the Scouts arrived, and had gone in the direction of Papinville or north. There was no enemy seen by the scouts. Day very pleasant.

Sunday, May 8. . . . We had some rain today. This evening I visited Mrs. R. Sergt. W. D. Porter went with me to spend the evening with Miss Alice. I have nothing more to mention of today. *(May 9 is omitted.)*

Tuesday, May 10. There was a heavy rain fall all last night. This morning a portion of our stables fell and one horse was badly injured thereby. The rain continued to fall in torrents all this forenoon. Afternoon the storm ceased and cleared off. The Marmaton river is rising rapidly. . . .

Wednesday, May 11. This morning the Marmaton was 30 feet deep and running out of its banks over the bottom lands. Jas H. Williams[1] a recruit while crossing a deep slough came near being drowned by falling from his horse, and some of the boys rescued him from a tree he took refuge in. We had a heavy frost last night. I finished my Pay Rolls today. . . .

1. Private James H. Williams, Baraboo, Wis.

Thursday, May 12. The Marmaton river commenced falling today, but is tearing away through the country yet at a fearful rate. This morning early we heard some cannonading but was unable to tell in what direction. I have been taking a rest today, and feel it a great relief after so long a siege of writing. . . .

Friday, May 13. The river fell very fast today and we was able to get communication from Fort Scott today. We learn that Genl. Grants forces had a terrific fight with Genl. Lees confederate force and came out victorious[1] which news is encouraging. . . .

1. The Spotsylvania campaign, May 7-19, is generally considered a successful Confederate defense, though it revealed to Lee Grant's determination to persevere despite frightful losses.

Sunday, May 15. I had Co. Inspection at 9 O'clock A.M. and seen that all was in proper order for the last scouting of the District Inspector whom we expect today. Afternoon Capt. Rees District Inspection arrived and inspected my Company and quarters and credited us with cleanliness and good discipline and he bear a good record of us to Hd. Qrs. he would [sic]. After a short stay with us he departed on his way to Co. "A" at Balltown. I took my departure about the same time to Mrs. R. to inspect her good looks, which was an agreeable trek. Day warm and pleasant.

Monday, May 16. This morning early we received news of the notorious Bushwhackers Capt. Henry Taylor[1] having been in the neighborhood during the night with 42 men and captured Joe Ury a scout at his fathers but Joe escaped after knocking one of his captors down with a club. Old man Ury was shot in the thigh by Taylors men and they soon departed.[2] Co. "D" 3rd Wis. Cav. and a Co. of 15th Kans. Cav. soon pursued and skirmished with them, and 25 men of my Co. in Comd. of Lieut. Willsey joined in pursuit. Co. "D" and 15 Kans. had two men wounded and guerrillas escaped with some loss. Day very warm.

1. See July 16, 1862 note. The "man of great ability" has now become "notorious" in Porter's eyes.

2. For extensive details concerning this dramatic raid and the incident at Urys', see *The History of Vernon County, Mo.* (1887), 322. Taylor and his men gave an account of Ury's escape less creditable to him. At the end of the chase the guerrillas reported one man badly wounded, two slightly.

Tuesday, May 17. I have not been very busy today. Sergt. John Donshoe[1] and 19 men returned to Company today from Escort to Supply Train to Fort Gibson, April 25th inst. They killed 5 guerrillas while gone. There was 25 Texas Refugees met and joined them on the trip for better protection, as they were in a sad and destitute condition from their long journeying, and having lost many of their number in fights with guerrillas on the journey. The poor fellows feel safe in Fort Scott. . . . *(May 18 is omitted.)*

1. Sergeant John Donahue, Cazenovia, Wis.

Thursday, May 19. This morning I took 20 men of my Company and went in hunt of the guerrillas. Henry Taylor and party who are reported in the neighborhood of Nevada. I went east ten miles and then turned south four miles near Nevada when I came upon a small portion of Taylors men, when we pursued and fired on them as they made quick time in their retreat. We followed them until we lost sight of them, when we abandoned farther pursuit. There was none killed that we discovered. . . .

Friday, May 20. There has been great excitement among the citizens in the neighborhood on account of the hordes of guerrillas having appeared of late, as they consider their lives and property in peril. We are using all the necessary means in our possession to make it too d----d uncomfortable for guerrillas to tarry long enough to eat a square meal in our locality. We are quietly awaiting events today. Today quite hot. *(May 21 is omitted.)*

Sunday, May 22. . . . At noon I rode up to Mr. Evans to spend the afternoon. I found all very well, and I enjoyed my visit with my lady friend Mrs. Rowntree until 5 O'clock when I returned to Camp to conduct Dress Parade after which Capt. Carpenter came and stayed through the night with us. Today very warm. *(May 23 is omitted.)*

Tuesday, May 24. This morning I sent my Scout John White in company with private Wm. Stoner, H. M. Russell, and Bart Kivell to Old town Branch[1] 6 miles north east of Nevada on a reconnoiter. On arriving near there they suddenly came upon Henry Taylor when a lively skirmish began and Taylors party was soon put to flight, there was none hurt as far as known, and all my men came safe to camp. I was idle today. . . . *(May 25-26 are omitted.)*

1. Old Town Branch, named after the Big Osage Indian

"old town" (ca. 1776-1824), rises a little northeast of Nevada and flows north by northwest into the Marmaton River.

Friday, May 27. Lieut. Willsey in command of 25 men started on a scout below Nevada and found all quiet and no enemy, and they spent the day scouting over the country and returned to Camp at dark. . . .

Saturday, May 28. All quiet on our lines today, the belief is that the guerrillas are not liable to stay here long when they come, as they prefer more quiet retreats and no interruptions while carrying on their nefarious business. I would say that Henry Taylor was Sheriff of Vernon Co. Mo. at the breaking out of our war. Alas how the mighty have fallen. Another hot day.

Sunday, May 29. I conducted our Company Inspection at 9 O'clock A.M. after which I concluded to spend the day with my widow friend Mrs. R----, so I saddle old Dick and was soon on the road and at the house of my lady where I remained until 5 O'clock P. M. when I returned to Camp to attend Dress Parade. I had a delightful time at my friends house, though the day was very hot, I hardly take notice of it as my attention was absorbed in the company of Mrs. R----.

Monday, May 30. This morning I took 2 [20?] men of Company and went on a scout in the vicinity of Shanghai, Pleasant Run and Nevada. I found all quiet and no enemy on our route. We arrived in camp at 5 O'clock P.M. after a march of 50 miles today. All seems to be very quiet on our beat at this time. . . .

Tuesday, May 31. . . . There is a large amount of business now in our Army Department and indications are that this year will convince the Rebels that they have no business in Missouri, for they can't get her, and they are fast being driven in their last ditch. Today very sultry and signs of more rain. *(June 1-2 are omitted.)*

Friday, June 3. All were idle in camp this forenoon. This afternoon I sent Sergt. Cooper in command of 20 men on a scout down Marmaton River. John White and Harrington two Scouts accompanied them. We had our usual Dress Parade at 5 O'clock P.M. Day very warm.

Saturday, June 4. The Scout came upon a company of 9 guerrillas in command of Bill Marchbanks this morning 6 miles from Camp. The boys surprised the guerrillas by falling upon them inspected and captured a fine horse from the Leader of the party and four more horses belonging to the men. The majority of the enemy escaped on foot as our men approached their camp, not being able to secure their horses, thus none were killed or captured. The boys are now building a Stockade around our camp making it more secure against the attack of a large force. Our Stockade is constructed of logs split into and set up perpendicular, with end deep into the ground and close together, the height being ten feet. Our Veteran

Recruits returned to Company today from Furlough in Wisconsin. They report having a good time at home and on their journey, and whipped all who opposed them in any way. I spent a horrible night with mosquitoes which were so numerous as to deprive one of sleep. Today very hot.

Sunday, June 5. I took charge of our Company Inspection this morning at 9 O'clock after which I rode out to visit Mrs. Rowntree where I had a very enjoyable visit and a good dinner with my lady friend. At 5 O'clock P.M. I returned to camp to command our Company Parade. The day has been sultry with an accompaniment of thunder and signs of rain. There was rain this evening. Capt. Carpenter stayed with us tonight, on his way to Fort Scott.

Monday, June 6. I have been busy doing our Company writing today, such as Tri Monthly Report and consolidated Report of Company. Lieut. Willsey took command of 25 men and went on a scout in the vicinity of Lamar, Mo. . . .

Tuesday, June 7. I spent the forenoon writing up my Company Qr. Mr. Returns. Mrs. Sample sent me an invitation to take dinner with her today, so I started out at noon in company with Private Wm. H. Stoner to Mrs. S----s Residence and found the fascinating widow had everything in fine order for our reception. After a few remarks we were invited to set down and partake of a royal good dinner which I will try to mention in part consisting of green peas, lettuce, gooseberry pie, cake, strawberries and cream. Well the widow came near capturing me by first foundering me. After dinner we had a good visit with our Host and daughter Dosia. Capt. Vittum went to the Fort on business this afternoon. Day warm. . . .

Wednesday, June 8. . . . Bro. W. D. Porter and command returned from Train Escort to Ft. Gibson. They killed 2 guerrillas while gone, but had no interruption from any large force so they succeeded in getting the Train through safe. Capt. Vittum was again compelled to go to the Fort today on business. Day very warm. *(June 9-13 are omitted.)*

Tuesday, June 14. . . . Capt. Vittum and Sergt. Cooper went to Judge Harvey Requas and took dinner today which the Captain pronounced his judgment on as the best dinner of the season. Day very warm. *(June 15-16 are omitted.)*

Friday, June 17. This morning my brother Sergt. W. D. Porter in command of 25 men of Co. joined Capt. Carpenter and Co. "A" of our Regt and started on a scout in the vicinity of Carthage and Clear Creek. I have not been busy today. Lieut. Willsey and Comd returned last evening from Scout, and report all quiet on their journey. Today terrible warm. *(June 18-23 are omitted.)*

Friday, June 24. . . . Sergt. W. D. Porter

returned with scouting party today after an absence of nearly 8 days and a march of 240 miles and an engagement with 300 of the enemy at Clear Creek, Mo. killing and wounding some, but the exact amount was not ascertained. Our boys escaped with but few slightly wounded. The enemy retreated in confusion leaving some horses which our boys captured. Day very hot.

Saturday, June 25. . . . Sergt. E. M. Cooper and 40 men in command of Capt. Vittum started on a scout southward this afternoon. Privates E. H. Rogers and Robert Pierce[1] bade us all farewell and took their departure this morning to Fort Scott to be sent to Reserve Veteran Corps. There was a slight shower today which was refreshing. . . . *(June 26 is omitted.)*

1. Robert Pierce, Baraboo, Wis.

Monday, June 27. This morning I took command of 25 men and some wagons and went to Nevada to get lumber for completion of our stable. While at Nevada I sent out a portion of my men to reconnoiter the vicinity, and they found no enemy. We found sufficient lumber to load our wagons, and returned to camp in due time. On my returned [sic] I stopped at Judge Requas and took dinner and finished my repast with cherry pie. *(June 28-30 are omitted.)*

Friday, July 1. . . . I received a letter this evening from my friend Julia Purdy in Baraboo, Wis. which was a treat as it furnished one very interesting news from home and friends. Today has been very hot.

Saturday, July 2. . . . Our Asst Surgeon Wm. H. Warner, wife and two little daughter took dinner with me today. They was on their way from Fort Scott to Balltown to visit Co. "A." The doctor has a very amiable wife and interesting children. After dinner they went to Balltown. Day very hot. *(July 3 is omitted.)*

Monday, July 4. This morning early our ears caught the sound of the cannons boom at Fort Scott reminding us that our National holy day had arrived. We got out our 12 pound Brass Mountain Howitzer and fired a compliment of shots that awoke the neighborhood and informed the guerrillas that Uncle Sam had a squad of energetic humanity ready for business at Fort Insley and prepared to visit the temporary abodes of guerrillas at any time without invitation, but we usually have a little show of formality on approaching their abodes which is disgusting to them. We had out a heavy Patrol on the lines today. I was thus engaged. Day very hot.

Tuesday, July 5. Last evening a portion of our Company that left camp under command of Capt. Vittum returned. They report that they went as escort to a Train to within 25 miles of Fort Gibson. Yesterday morning they was attacked by about 400 of the enemy at Cow Creek.[1] Our entire force was 82 men. After a lively little fight in which one horse of any [our]

Company was wounded and some of the enemy was surrounded his little force so he ordered a retreat which was conducted in an orderly manner for a distance of 12 miles and frequent skirmishing in which the enemy lost a number and withdrew from the contests. Capt. Vittum thinks he was fortunate in bringing his men out safe considering the numbers of the enemy. Today very warm. *(July 6-9 are omitted.)*

1. Cow Creek, a tributary of Spring River, in eastern Crawford and Cherokee counties, Kansas.

Sunday, July 10. . . . I learn this morning that my friend Mrs. R---- whom I will in the future take the liberty to call Bettie was quite sick. I sent Sergt. Wm. Ridings[1] in command of 23 men on a scout this morning. There was a light shower this evening. . . .

1. First Sergeant William Ridings, Baraboo, Wis.

Monday, July 11. . . . I rode out this afternoon to see friend Bettie. I found her quite unwell, also her sister Alice and three small children, were down with chills and fever. The place had the appearance of a general hospital. I remained a short time and rendered what assistance I could and returned to camp. . . .

Tuesday, July 12. . . . Sergt. Ridings returned from Scout this forenoon. They report having a fight at Horse Creek with about 3 [30?] guerrillas killing 3 and wounding some. Our boys was fortunate in securing 5 horses and equipments and put the rascals to flight. Capt. Vittum went to the Fort today prior to going to Wis. on 20 days leave of absence. The day very hot.

Wednesday, July 13. At one O'clock this morning I took 15 men and went in the vicinity of Nevada in search of guerrillas I believed was there. At 9 O'clock I came upon 6 of the enemy who fired upon us without serious results, we then charged upon them fired on them and killed two when the others escaped. We secured 3 good horses and returned to camp at noon. We had a heavy shower this afternoon. . . .

Thursday, July 14. This morning our old Negro waiter Joe bade us good bye and took his departure for Wisconsin. I was not very busy beyond attending to the calls of citizens who frequently visit us. The day has been terrible hot.

Friday, July 15. I have been busy at work on my Pay Rolls and desperately fighting flies and mosquitos which continually bite and sting us day and night, and remind us that the Devils dominions are located at this place, or his imps in miniature form are on a tour of inspection. . . . *(July 16-18 are omitted.)*

Tuesday, July 19. We are trying to find cool places today to escape the oppressive heat which is intolerable besides Mosquitoes and flies continually torment us day and night, and a very minute insect which is too small to be seen with ordinary sight, and are an inhabitant of vegetation, they get on the skin of a person and cause such burning and itching as to deprive one of sleep or rest. They are called Chigoes.[1] We are of the opinion that every foot of hell is here exhibited and we have free tickets.

1. *Tunga penetrans,* called the "chigger" by Missourians, to whom it is an old if unpleasant acquaintance.

Wednesday, July 20. I took 20 men of my Company and started from camp at 3 O'clock this morning to reconnoiter the country south east of Nevada. At about 10 O'clock A.M. we discovered a camp of guerrillas numbering 34 in a dense woods on Clear Creek. I soon laid out my course to pursue in making the attack, all being ready we made a furious charge taking the enemy by surprise who fired but few shots and fled leaving 7 of their number dead on the spot and 11 horses as trophies of our success besides 4 good Saddles and 3 Double barrel guns, 6 Remington Revolvers. I spent the day scouting the country here and meeting no more of the enemy. I returned to camp at dark. The day was terrible hot and dry.

Thursday, July 21. I have been feeling quite unwell today. I presume it caused by yesterdays heat and fatigue. Some of my men who accompanied me are complaining of pain in their heads and a general debility of the system. I sent the captured horses and other property to Fort Scott today to be turned over to the Quarter Master and get Receipt for same. All is a scene of indolence and quiet in camp today, and terrible hot and oppressing.

Friday, July 22. I have symptoms of chills and fever this morning and consequently feel dilapidated and unfit for duty. This evening I sent a scout of 20 men and Sergeant in command to Montevallo. The days continue hot and nights cool.

Saturday, July 23. I am not feeling any better today, and ague symptoms continue to receive reinforcements and invest my position, and I conclude that the attack is near at hand. Not being acquainted with the tactics of this kind of an enemy I find myself wholly unprepared with the proper ammunition, and likely I may find a lively time in ridding myself of his presence. There is nothing important with us today. Very hot.

Sunday, July 24. I felt some better this morning and attended to inspecting my Company at 9 O'clock, after which I rode out to visit Bettie. At noon I was attacked with a chill, which was an unwelcome visitor especially at this time. Immediately the fever came on and lasted nearly all the afternoon, after which I returned to camp, at which time the Scout that went from Camp on Friday last returned and report having an engagement on yesterday at Montevallo with a large Guerrilla band killing two of the Enemy, and capturing 12 horses which they brought in camp. Our boys luckily escaped injury. Today very hot.

Monday, July 25. I have not been well today, and felt like chills had laid siege upon me. I shall make out a requisition for ammunition[1] to combat the late enemy (chills.) There has been no disturbance of an unusual character today. The weather continues terrible hot, with very cool nights.

1. Presumably preparations containing quinine, in early days called "Peruvian bark." Its use in treating malaria was recognized from Spanish colonial times, and was introduced in frontier Missouri in American times by Dr. John Sappington of Arrow Rock, but it was often in short supply.

Tuesday, July 26. I am prepared for the conflict. Having a premonition that the chills would renew the attack yesterday, so I opened the fight with a large dose of Hostetters Bitters before Breakfast, after breakfast I took some Ague Pills, the formula was quinine and Strychnine, equal to 29 parts of the former and 1 of the latter. I then took a large drink of Cherry Brandy, shortly after I drank one quart of Buttermilk, and escaped the attack of chills today. Today very hot.

Wednesday, July 27. I rode out to my friend Betties this morning and enjoyed a few hours pleasant talk, and felt better otherwise by having no chill symptoms. While here I received a Dispatch from Fort Scott which announced that Quantrell with a large guerrilla force was near Paola, Kans.[1] and I was ordered to put out a strong Patrol in connection with other troop on the line. I returned to camp and sent out some men immediately on the look out. Very warm today.

1. Paola, in Miami County, Kan., was headquarters of the Federal Department of Kansas.

Thursday, July 28. Lieut. Willsey went to Fort Scott this morning for farther instruction as too our patrol duties and the ground we are to occupy. I sent out Sergt Porter in command of Patrol this morning, with orders to pass between our camp and Patosi, Kans.[1] I have not been very busy today. Lieut Willsey returned from the Fort this evening. All reported quiet on our lines today. Day very hot. *(July 29 is omitted.)*

1. Potosi, a township in east central Linn County, Kansas, on the Missouri border, including present Pleasanton.

Saturday, July 30. The enemy is still reported hovering near us, as he has been seen frequently near the Kans. Border of late, and the supposition is he will try to make a dash on some point in Kansas before many days. Our Patrol is on the look out today, between our Camp and Patosi, Kans. . . .

Sunday, July 31. . . . After inspection I rode out to spend a portion of the day with my true friend Bettie, where I spent the few hours of my stay in the most satisfactory manner and I find my visits here are a great relief from the cares and vexations incident to the command of a company and various duties connected therewith, besides a little time spent in ladies company I find very profitable and refining with those whose business is to deal with a Company of rough men of all classes of society. All quiet on our lines today. The day has been cloudy and cool with some rain. My friend Capt. Carpenter stopped with me to night. . . .

Monday, August 1. I have been quite busy today making up my Monthly Return of Company to be forwarded to the Adjutant General, State of Wisconsin. The troops so far have not come in contact with the notorious Quantrell, and we are again resuming our careless habits and withdrawn our Patrol as we learn that Quantrell has gone to Jackson Co. Mo. All quiet here and we are the kind to keep the neighborhood quiet or make a terrible racket. Today has been quite pleasant. *(Aug. 2-5 are omitted.)*

Saturday, August 6. This morning there was a large concourse of the citizens of Vernon County, Mo. met at our camp to make arrangements where by civil laws[1] might be again established in the county. I took no interest in their proceedings, any more than witness a fight between two of the citizens which resulted in one of the twain carrying home a face terribly dilapidated. I have been very busy writing on my Company papers today. I received a dispatch from Capt. Carpenter for 15 men and one Sergeant to join a portion of his Company on a Scout at Montevallo this evening. The required number was sent in command of Sergt. Stansfield. Day very warm.

1. Martial law had existed throughout Missouri since August 20, 1861. Lincoln's suspension of habeas corpus on Sept. 24, 1862, effectively placed all the United States under martial law. "It is really no law at all, but rather the supplanting of existing laws by the orders of a military commander."—Henry V. Poor, advisory editor, *You and the Law,* Pleasantville, N.Y., Readers Digest Assn., 1971, 76.

Sunday, August 7. This morning Capt. Vittum went to Fort Scott on business. Reports from our Scouts are that they had a desperate encounter with a band of Guerrillas at an early hour this morning. Two of the enemy was killed and some were wounded. Two of our boys of Co. "A" was wounded. One in the breast, and the other in the thigh. The Scout returned to camp this evening, bring in the wounded. I visited friend Bettie today, and had a very pleasant visit. . . .

Tuesday, August 8. I sent the wounded in an ambulance to the Hospital at Fort Scott for medical and surgical treatment. My time was taken up today in writing a Military History of my Company. There was nothing very Important that farther transpired with us today. The day was very warm.

Tuesday, August 9. I have been quite busy writing up my Co. history today, which is to be sent to the Adjutant General, State of Wisconsin. My Company is in very good health, and good fighting condition, ready for business when required, and never known to retreat or show the white feather. Our motto is no quarters to Bushwhackers or guerrillas. I have nothing beyond our usual camp duties to mention today. Day very hot. *(Aug. 10-12 are omitted.)*

Saturday, August 13. This morning Alexander Preston,[1] a member of my Company took a widow Woodruff[2] a neighbor and went to Fort Scott where they were united in marriage, and returned to the Brides Residence where a fine supper was prepared, and I being invited drew my share of the Rations. After supper I was drawn into a frolic with the Misses Florence Requa, Mary Daugherty, Dosia Sample, and Angie Snelson.[3] Water was issued freely and we presented a bedrabled appearance at the end of the spree, however we enjoyed our sport with good will. There being a good number present, a dance was soon started, all present taking part. During the evening a number of the Company and citizens brought the festivities to a stop, by a sudden pandemonium of discordant sounds produced by cow bells, horns, Tin-pans and other instruments,[4] but the dance, soon took up the step to more harmonious music which continued until near day, when I went to camp. Day very warm. *(Aug 14-15 are omitted.)*

1. Private Alexander Preston, Appleton, Wis.

2. Presumably the widow either of Captain Alexander Woodruff, who settled near Deerfield in 1836, or of his invalid son Marcus, both of whom were murdered by Kansans in March, 1862.—*History of Vernon County,* 311, 519.

3. Angeline, 15, dau. of Sarah V. Snelson, Deerfield Twp.

4. A shivaree, from French *charivari,* the folk custom of hurrahing a newlywed couple on their bridal night.

Tuesday, August 16. This morning I took 20 men of my Co. and started on a scout. I went down Marmaton river ten miles without discovering the enemy. I then took a direction toward Horse Creek, and after a march of five miles I discovered two men riding towards some timber. I immediately inspected the locality and found a camp of 25 or 30 Guerrillas. I soon had my men ready for action and charged their camp, and was greeted by a volley of bullets and buck shot which produced no serious results except slightly wounding one horse and flying about us in close proximity. Before they could escape we had four of their number rolling up their eyes and turning up their toes. We captured 6 horses and equipments, 4 guns and 3 good Revolvers, the remainder made their escape, we pursued them but was unable to come upon them during the day. We camped near Little Osage river tonight. Day very hot. *(Aug. 17-24 are omitted.)*

Tuesday, August 25. We learn this morning that some guerrillas are camped on Clear Creek, but report is not reliable. We expect correct statements before taking action in the matter. We are prepared to move on the enemy at any time. Fine weather today.

Friday, August 26. We are in receipt of news today that a large camp of guerrillas are assembling on Clear Creek which confirms reports already at hand. I conclude to go in search of them. So at 2 O'clock this afternoon I took 24 men from my Company and started by way of Nevada and at dark I found the enemy was in Camp three miles distant. I thought proper to camp and at daylight take a careful observation of their position before making the attack. I did so, and found about 40 of the enemy in a dense woods. I made my arrangements for an immediate attack. I divided my command and gave my Sergt. Leonard P. Luce charge of one detachment while I took charge of the other and charged on the enemy. Fine day.

Saturday, August 27. As above stated I matured my plans, at an early hour, and at about 5 O'clock this morning we attacked the camp from two points and took the guerrillas by surprise who made but little resistance. We killed seven and suppose wounded many but was unable to learn how many, the remainder made a rapid retreat, leaving a quantity of camp equipage and 11 horses and some guns and revolvers which we took in. We found the enemy so scattered that pursuit was considered of but little profit. We are of the opinion that our loss would have been many had we not surprised them, but we escaped with few close calls. The fight took place about 5 miles from the town of Montevallo. We spent the day scouting over the country and camped at dark without finding any more of the enemy to disturb and give us a little excitement. But we feel repaid for our risk and trip. We camped 6 miles east of Nevada and took our remaining ration of Hard-tack and lay down for rest as both men and horses was fatigued a great deal. Today warm and pleasant.

Sunday, August 28. This morning at 5 O'clock

we started for camp 14 miles distant, and our Rations having played out, the prospects were that no breakfast could be had until we reached camp. We arrived at camp at 8 O'clock this morning. I sent in a report of my success to Hd. Quarters at Fort Scott soon after my arrival at camp. After dinner I rode out to spend the afternoon at Mr. Evans with friend Bettie and her two sisters Misses Angie and Alice. I spent two or three hours very agreeable with the ladies and returned to camp in due time for conducting Dress Parade. Today has been pleasant. *(Aug. 29-Sept. 8 are omitted.)*

Friday, September 9. . . . We are in receipt of news that some guerrillas are east of us fifteen miles, but think they are trying to escape out of the country. Today warm and pleasant.

Saturday, Sept. 10. I find myself quite rested this morning and I hardly know what to employ my time at today. After I partook of a good breakfast I walked over to Judge Harvey Requas and spent the forenoon very pleasantly with him and family and especially with his daughter Miss Florence, a very estimable lady. I took dinner with them and fared sumptuously. After dinner I returned to camp where I spent the remainder of the day. . . . *(Sept. 11 is omitted.)*

Monday, September 12. Today I have not been very busy. My Capt. David S. Vittum accompanied by 1st Lieut. J. B. Pond of Co. "C" 3rd Wis. Cav. came to our camp during the day. My Capt presented me with my Commission as 1st Lieut. of Co. "F" 3rd Wis. Cav. And he also presented a commission to Sergt Eli M. Cooper as 2nd Lieut. of same Company. Well as it is the custom in the army on such occasions, was, a little of the mysterious creatures known by names very numerous was brought into requisition, I being supplied with the article late from the commissary department. We all partook of the contents of a Demijohn and then had a good supper set before us by my cook Willis A. Hawes.[1] The Captain and Lieutenant gave me credit for being so fortunate in securing so good a cook. Today very pleasant.

1. Private Willis A. Hawes, Kilbourn City, Wis.

Tuesday, September 13. This morning Sergeant Cooper and myself rode to Fort Scott to be Mustered as Lieutenants. I was Mustered by Major W. C. Ransom to date from today as 1st Lieut. of Co. "F" 3rd Regt Wis. Cav. Sergt. Cooper not being supplied with the requisite papers, his muster was postponed until he could produce them. After we spent some time in the Fort we returned to our Company, and arrived duly sober and without accident. Today pleasant.

Wednesday, September 14. I received a dispatch early this morning from Fort Scott directing me to send out a Patrol in the country as small bodies of the enemy were again in our locality. I sent out two parties in Patrol through the country and learn the facts. At dark my patrol came in and reported that they did not see any enemy, but learned that there had been some seen by citizens. Today very pleasant.

Thursday, September 15. I sent out Patrols again today, and took a squad of men and went below Nevada three miles, and at two O'clock P.M. I came upon a party of nine guerrillas in a small timber strip whom we attacked but did not succeed in capturing but two whom we fortunately killed when we first attacked the camp, the others escaped. We captured the horses and the arms the two men possessed and left the two men for the wolves and buzzards to hold a grand feast over. I took a north course three miles, and then returned to my Company at dark without loss or incident. My other Patrol report all quiet on their rounds. Today pleasant. *(Sept. 16 is omitted.)*

Saturday, September 17. I learn from my Pickets this morning that all was quiet on the line last night. After breakfast I sent out my Patrol as usual. I keep enough force in camp repel any ordinary force that would presume to attack us, as we are well fortified to resist an attack from superior numbers. . . . Some of the Patrol report seeing a small party of the enemy five miles from camp, but they were in full retreat when discovered. . . . *(Sept. 18-19 are omitted.)*

Tuesday, Sept. 20. This morning Major Ross[1] and Lieut Beam[2] stopped at our Camp in their return to Fort Scott, they made a short stay with us. We received intelligence today that the army supply train enroute to Fort Gibson Cherokee Nation was captured yesterday morning at Cabin Creek, C.N. by 3000 Rebels. We did not get the full particulars. Today quiet, mild and warm. *(Sept. 21-23 are omitted.)*

1. Major E. J. Ross, district inspector.
2. Post adjutant at Fort Scott.

Saturday, September 24. *(At Fort Scott)* I received orders to prepare my company for grand Review, and this forenoon was occupied in the necessary preparation. At 2 O'clock P.M. all the troops comprising the 1st Sub District of Kansas was Reviewed by Colonel C. R. Jennison[1] of 15th Kans. Cavalry, commanding 1st Sub. Dist. The display of Military and citizens was a grand spectacle, as usual. We had a very dusty and disagreeable day.

1. Charles R. "Doc" Jennison, "Jennison the Jayhawker."

Sunday, September 25. . . . At about noon I received orders to return with my Company to my former camp (Insley). Companies "A", "D" & "C" of my Regiment also received orders to return to their former camps. The men soon packed up our baggage and was in readiness to move. The boys were pleased with the prospect of again returning to their former camp as they did not like the idea of remaining on duty at Fort Scott. We soon moved on our way to our destination. I stopped at friend Betties and partook of a good supper while my Company went on to camp. I remained with friend Bettie during the evening and was royally entertained. . . . *(Sept. 26 is omitted.)*

Tuesday, September 27. I deemed it necessary to be on my guard, as information comes in that bands of the enemy have been seen in our vicinity, of late, and commanders of troops have been ordered to keep a vigilant guard against surprise. I sent out a Patrol to discover if possible if any enemy was liable to give us a little entertainment. After a thorough investigation no enemy was discovered, and the Patrol arrived in camp at dark. Captain Carpenter came to our camp this evening on his way to Fort Scott and stopped with me during the night. All quiet with us today. . . .

Wednesday, September 28. I sent out another Patrol in conjunction with other Companies on the border, as we are determined to be found ready for the jig when the music commences. All reported quiet on our lines today. Pleasant weather today.

Thursday, September 29. I sent out my scouts again this morning as we are informed that the confederate forces in Arkansas are contemplating a raid in Missouri under command of Generals Price and Marmaduke and the bands of the Enemy seen of late are supposed to be recruits, or advance of Prices Army. This we are in expectation of having as lively job on hand soon. I have spent the day writing up some Company papers which gives me but little leisure time to do Scouting at this time. . . .

Friday, September 30. I concluded to see a little of the outside world this morning, so I saddled old Dick and rode out to see my friend Bettie, where her sister Angie informed me that B--- was engaged at washing by the River Marmaton near by. Well I was aware that women were not in a pleasant state of mind on occasions of wash days, so I was about to return to camp without a chat, but Miss Angie told me to see Bettie before I returned, I rode out to the place and found Bettie quite cheerful, so I spent a few moments of conversation with her, and rode back to camp. I then spent the day writing. . . . *(Oct. 1-2 are omitted.)*

Monday, October 3. . . . Today very stormy and the Marmaton river near our camp is raising very fast. We are informed that the confederate forces under Genl Price have entered Missouri,[1] so we are on the watch for the advance of his army. My Scouts can't cross the river tonight.

1. Price's Confederates, some 12,000 strong, entered southeast Missouri on September 16.

Tuesday, October 4. We are in receipt of a dispatch from Fort Scott this morning informing us that Genl Sterling Price and force of 1700 men was in the vicinity of Pilot Knob, Mo. and had an engagement with Genl Ewing at that point in which the latter was defeated. I was directed to keep my men in readiness and guard against surprise and keep a scout out to guard against the enemy committing depredations in our midst. I succeeded in getting a Scouting party across the Marmaton this morning which was attended with great danger to men and horses as the river was bank full and strong current. There was great excitement prevailing among the citizens on account of the news. Today very stormy.

Wednesday, October 5. There was great excitement prevailing in both military and civil circles today. Our army here are busy preparing for the coming conflict, and anxious to test the question of who must get out of Missouri, or Kansas be devastated by the enemy. The weather still stormy.

Thursday, October 6. Today clear and pleasant all signs of more rain have disappeared. The excitement continues to increase as reports come in from the enemy. The news by Telegraph report Price having attacked Jefferson City, but we doubt the report as true. My Scout report on their return this evening that no enemy was seen. I rode out to my friend B----s this afternoon. . . . *(Oct. 7 is omitted.)*

Saturday, October 8. Fighting continues at Jefferson City but the enemy are cognizant of the fact that they have a large[r] contract to fill than they expected. All is quiet with us today. I received an order to report without delay to C. S. Charlott Asst. Adj. Genl. at Fort Leavenworth, Kans. for duty. I made all necessary preparations to start on Monday. Today pleasant. *(Oct. 9 is omitted.)*

Monday, October 10. I received an order from Head Quarters Fort Scott directing me to report with my Company to the Fort this morning or during the day with Camp equipage. At an early hour we was on the move, I stopped on my way at Betties until near noon, when I bade my friend good bye until we should meet again, and then hastened on my journey arriving at the Fort at 2 O'clock P.M. Today pleasant.

On the 11th Porter set off alone by stagecoach to Fort Leavenworth. On the 12th the coach, "having on board 24 passengers," overturned near Olathe, though without injuries. He arrived at Leavenworth late on the 12th.

Friday, October 14. I received orders during the night from Capt. Williams acting Asst. Adjt. Genl. ordering me to take passage on steamboat Emily and report to Maj. Charlott Asst. Ajt. Genl. at Wyandotte, Kans. for duty. I arrived at Wyandotte at 12½ O'clock P.M. and reported at Genl. Saml Curtis Hd Qrs. to Maj. C. S. Charlott who assigned me to duty as Actg Asst Qr Master and Commissary at Wyandotte. I immediately took charge of the Stores at the landing and procured some colored troops to store them in a building. I had several barrels of whiskey of which I supplied my dusky help bountifully, and a jolly crew I soon had. Late in the night we completed our task. Troops are constantly arriving and pass on to the front. Price is near Lexington today, and advancing on Kansas City, as there is a small force to interfere in his advance he moves rapidly. Today pleasant, some sign of rain.

Tuesday, October 18. There was heavy skirmishing near Independence Mo. today as reported by some of my Company who were engaged, and whom I saw this evening. Our troops are massing on the Little Blue river and are going to give the Johnnies a check. Troops are hurrying to the front, and the citizens of Wyandotte[1] and Kansas City are wild with excitement. I have been busy as usual all day issuing Commissary and quarter Master Stores and I have no idle time. . . .

1. Wyandott City (sic), future Kansas City, Kans., was incorporated in 1859.

Wednesday, October 19. . . . I have heard cannonading all day, and messengers arrive with reports of heavy fighting on the Blue river near Kansas City. I feel a desire to be there, but I supposed my services are as necessary here for the support of those at the front. We continue to have fine weather.

Thursday, October 20. . . . There was a rain and sleet commenced falling quite early, but continued only a short time when it cleared off and we had a pleasant day. There was some considerable skirmishing today on the Blue but no general engagement. Excitement has not abated here or at Kas. City.

Friday, October 21. This day has been cool and stormy. But the fighting continues today by the Blue and Price is anxious to enter Kansas City by the shortest and easiest route, but he finds it a hard road to travel. . . . I spent a portion of the day in town, and was introduced to a young lady, by name Mary Brown, who I found by conversation, of good education besides she was very beautiful. Though she informed me that she was of the Wyandotte Indian tribe. But I had a very interesting conversation with her and was invited to dine with her and her parents who are wealthy residents of Wyandotte.

Saturday, October 22. There was a heavy battle took place today, and the cannonading and musketry was distinctly heard at this place. Our forces were drove back to the vicinity of Westport five miles south of Kansas City, here the battle raged until dark, without any decisive results. I was forced to remain at my post of duty unable to take an active part with my comrades at the front. I learn that the enemy lost very heavy today, but our loss was small in comparison. . . .

Sunday, October 23. *(Porter started for the battle scene on a dilapidated horse.)* I overlook a Regiment of Militia in command of Col. Veal from Topeka, Kan. I fell in with the Regt. and rode on to Westport and then to a crossing on the Blue, when we was attacked by overwhelming force of the enemy, which threw these raw troops in a panic and about one half of the Regiment was captured. I succeeded in making my escape in a field, followed by fifteen of the enemy a distance of half a mile who kept shooting, and calling on me to halt. Well, the bones I rode never faltered on the order of going at a fearful speed until he cleared the fence leaving our pursuers in the field a beating a poor negro with their revolvers. I found I was clear from farther pursuit, and having had glory enough for one day, I rode leisurely back to the City of Wyandotte. This evening we learn that the enemy are whipped and in full retreat. I received orders from Genl Curtis this evening to load Steamer Tom Morgan with a large quantity of Rations and send to Kans. City. I succeeded in loading the boat by midnight. . . .

Monday, October 24. We learn last night that the enemy was defeated yesterday in the afternoon after a severe battle below Westport. As soon as the battle ended the enemy commenced retreating south, their course being on the line of Missouri and Kansas. Our troops are in hot pursuit and taking many prisoners artillery, and a large quantity of army supplies and frequently attacking the rear of the enemy today. The excitement here has abated, and great joy mingled with sadness has taken its place. Some rain and sleet fell here last night, and today is quite stormy.

Tuesday, October 25. We learn today that our forces have had some severe engagements at the Trading Post[1] on the Kas. line, Mine Creek and Marmaton river, which engagements save Fort Scott from attack. The enemy camped tonight at Dry Wood twelve miles east of Fort Scott, here they destroyed over one hundred wagons heavy loaded with ammunition and captured goods.[2] I did not learn of any thing farther today. Today some cloudy but pleasant.

1. Trading Post, in northeast Linn County, Kan., took its name from a Chouteau post on the Marais des Cygnes River.

2. The final engagement of the day, the Battle of the Marmaton or the Battle of Charlot or Charlot Prairie, covering a wide area some two miles southwest of modern Richards, Mo., a successful rearguard action led by Shelby against a disorganized pursuit. The troops could cross the Marmaton at many fords but the wagon train only at Douglass Ford some six miles east (ironically the site of Porter's company's post, from which most of the troops had been withdrawn). The Confederates destroyed "about 500 wagons," says *The History of Vernon County,* 326.

Wednesday, October 26. We learn today that Genl. Marmaduke of the confederates was captured yesterday near Mine Creek by James Dunlavy of the 1st Iowa Cavalry. At 3 O'clock this morning the enemy left camp and our troops are making it uncomfortable for them in the extreme as they journey on. There is a large quantity of ammunition, arms of nearly all kinds left at the enemies camp, besides Wagons, Harness, horses, and various kinds of plunder left in their haste to get away from the Yankees who continually reminded them that destruction was on their road. Genl. [William] Rosecrans[1] has aided Generals Curtis and Blunt with a co-operative force under Genls [Alfred] Pleasanton,[2] Sanborn and [John] McNeil.[3] Last night was spent by our General disputing as to who had the right to the prisoner Marmaduke. It was decided that Pleasanton should take him in charge, and he starts for St. Louis this morning with his comd. Today pleasant.

1. Having quarreled with his Washington superiors and lost the Battle of Chickamauga, Major General William S.

Rosecrans was relieved and given command of the Department of Missouri, essentially an administrative job. His forces hung on Price's rear across Missouri.

2. Major General Alfred S. Pleasonton, the commander of the Federal cavalry at Gettysburg (July, 1863), was transferred to Missouri in March, 1864.

3. Brigadier General John McNeil, commanding a brigade of the Missouri State Militia, led the Federal pursuit in the Battle of Charlot.

Thursday, October 27. I learn that our forces camped last night 23 miles south of Fort Scott upon the road to Lamar, Mo. but have kept Old Pap Price on the move at a lively rate of speed and frequent skirmishes with our force that press their rear.

The excitement here a few days since,[1] has subsided and the people have resumed their usual occupations. I have plenty of leisure now, and occupy the time by reading and engaging in an occasional game of cards or billiards. I learn that my company is complimented very high by Genl. Blunt and others for their bravery and endurance in the various engagements and marches they have took part in during the campaign. I have just learned that Michael Kivel of my Co. was shot through cheek and mouth, and captured by the enemy near the Blue while fighting there. . . .

1. "All that day Ft. Scott had been in great alarm . . . the citizens . . . believed that if the place were captured it would be razed to the ground . . . a speculative person with $100 in cash could have bought and paid for the entire town. There was ground for uneasiness, for some scouting Confederates came within sight, and indeed Shelby's fine division was only 12 miles north of Ft.

Scott, advancing rapidly. . . ."—*The History of Vernon County,, 327.*

Friday, October 28. Reports are coming in from the front that there is prospects of a battle to take place at Newtonia, Mo., as the enemy seem to be concentrating their force of 26000 men at that point. Our Army in pursuit are designated as the Army of the Border. The 2nd Brigade to which my Company belongs was commanded by Col. Jennison of the 15th Kansas. The 1st Brigade by Col. Ford of the 2nd Colorado Cavalry. Our boys are whooping the Johnnies today and are near Lamar. All quiet here. . . .

Saturday, October 29. The report is this morning that our forces of the 1st and 2nd Brigades came upon the enemy at Newtonia[1] about 3 O'clock P.M. the 2nd Brigade being on the advance made the attack, when a desperate battle soon followed my Company with others of my Regiment who was in the Brigade showed they were business at once [sic] and held the enemy in check until reinforced, the enemy was again defeated by inferior numbers and a loss of 175 wounded, 35 seriously. Killed not known, only that two Colonels were killed. They also buried Gen. Harmmans, who was wounded at Mine Creek. Our loss is 95 wounded 18 killed and 1 missing. About 20 seriously wounded. About 100 horses killed or wounded. The 3rd Wis. Cav had 11 wounded, none killed. . . .

1. Newtonia is usually regarded as a Confederate victory.

Sunday, October 30. Our forces camped at Newtonia last night and the enemy have 35 seriously wounded in Hospital three miles south of Newtonia, and the enemies rear are at that point. Genl. Rosecrans withdrew Genls. Sandbörn and McNeil with their force, leaving Genls Curtis and Blunt too weak to do the enemy any damage, so Genl Curtis ordered his forces to return to Forts Scott and Leavenworth, at the time when we had the enemy within our grasp we are now compelled to retire before a defeated, demoralized seven times beaten foe. Thus ends this eventful campaign. It has been quiet in Wyandotte today. I do not enjoy this place, not enough excitement or energy here now to scare a fly off the end of a persons nose. . . .

Monday, October 31. This morning I took a walk up in town, and found many talking and congratulating each other on escaping the danger, that for two weeks seemed eminent [sic]. Some Kansas State Malitia passed through town today enroute home, as their services were no longer required. We now consider that all farther attempts of the Confederates to invade Missouri or Kansas, are at an end, except small bands of Gerrillas who are too cowardly to engage in honorable warfare, but display great bravery in robbing poor defenseless women, children and old men, frequently committing the most dastardly and fiendish outrages known to the warfare of the untutored savage.

Porter spent November in Wyandotte, observing the presidential election and complaining of disorders in "this city of Half breds, robbers, gamblers, murderers and drunkards."

Monday, November 28. . . . I was not busy at anything worthy of notice. This evening I was taken by surprise, happily so as the City hack drove up, having on board my friend Mrs. Bettie Rowntree and little daughter Mollie with whom I spent a pleasant evening. Bettie informed me of her fathers late marriage, and under these circumstances deemed it expedient to leave home and visit her sister Mollie Scruggs[1] at Independence, Mo. but was oblige to stop at this place until she could get conveyance to her sisters.

1. Neé Mary (sic) Evans, born Garrard County, Ky., June 5, 1838.

Tuesday, November 29. Today very cool. I spent a little time this morning in conversation with Bettie, and having been engaged to be united in marriage at the expiration of my term of Service, I at once realized the homeless condition of my friend, and proposed that we at once be united as man and wife, after due deliberation she consented to my proposition. I proceeded to Kans City to make the necessary preparations for the event. *(Nov. 29 is omitted.)*

Thursday, December 1. . . . I have arranged with the Proprietor Mr. Hallford[1] where I board, to furnish Bettie and daughter a good room which he has done, so Bettie is comfortable situated. Today has been quite cold. *(Dec. 2-3 are omitted.)*

1. Unidentified.

Sunday, December 4. I have spent the day out in town, occasionally stop in and converse with Bettie who seems to be quite cheerful. The day has been clear and pleasant, I had a friend accompany me to the residence of Revd R. D. Parker,[1] Pastor of the Congregational Church at this place. I engaged his services to unite Mrs. Bettie Rowntree and self in holy wedlock, which service was performed at 8 O'clock this evening in the east room of the Garno House,[2] Wyandotte, Kans. Robert Halford and wife Hester A. Halford and Ruth A. Noble were the guests present, witnesses of said marriage. After the usual congratulations the minister took his departure to fill his appointment and duties at church. Thus is added to my list of captures in army life the most valuable and greatest prize of all.

1. R. D. Parker became first pastor of the First Congregational Church of Wyandotte in 1859. "In March 1860 work commenced on a new church building, corner Fifth street and Nebraska avenue . . . completed in July and dedication held Aug. 1, 1860."—*Wyandotte County and Kansas City, Kan.*, 1890, 328-329.

2. "The old Garno House, at the northwest corner of Third Street and Minnesota Avenue, for many years was a famous hostelry."—Perl Wilbur Morgan, *History of Wyandotte County, Kansas, and its People.* Chicago, 1911, 339.

Porter spent December and early January continuing his commissary and quartermaster duties at Wyandotte, commenting on the severe weather and activities with his new wife, who visited her sister Mrs. Scruggs in Independence.

❦ 1865 ❦

Thursday, January 5. I received a letter from Bro. W. D. Porter of my Company today, and he informed me that all things relating to my Company are in a rather dilapidated condition, and the men are under loose discipline, under the command of 2nd Lieut. Eli W. Cooper. I presume I will have a task of some magnitude on my hands to bring the Company back to its former efficiency. . . . *(Jan. 6-15 are omitted.)*

Monday, January 16. . . . This afternoon I attended the trial of two disrespectable characters by name of Theodore Bartwell and Albert Savero. These men were on trial for robbing some household goods of Mrs. Toothman of Quindaro, a small town 6 or 7 miles from this City. The men were bound over to appear at next term of court. *(Jan. 17-23 are omitted.)*

Tuesday, January 24. I finished invoicing this forenoon and left them the stores in charge of the Lieutenant. I made preparations to take my departure this evening enroute to Fort Scott, Kas. Bettie and her daughter Mollie have been unwell with chills today. We rode over to Kansas City this evening and put up or stopped at the Gillis House for the night. . . .

Wednesday, January 25. This morning I bade wife and Mollie good bye as they were going to Independence, Mo. to wifes sister. I took passage on stage to Olathe,[1] Kas. Had a terribly cold ride, but by frequent potations of corn juice I managed to keep from freezing. I changed stage at Olathe and continued my journey, arrived at Paola, Kans. at 5 O'clock P.M. where we stopped for the night. I had a liberal supply of warming fluid, which the driver never refused to partake of. After a bountiful supper and warmth of a good fire, I turned in for a good sleep.

1. Seat of Johnson County, Kan.

Thursday, January 26. This morning at 4 O'clock I was again on my journey. The Stage was heavy loaded with passengers and baggage, and the weather intense cold, the lady passengers suffered a great deal. Took breakfast at Twin Springs[1] and soon after continued our journey. We the men were frequently obliged to take a run some distance to help the Kansas whiskey keep us from freezing. We divided such articles as we had with the ladies to keep them as comfortable as we could. We passed through Moneka[2] and Mound City[3] this forenoon. Took dinner at Fort Lincoln[4] at 2 O'clock P.M. arrived at Fort Scott at 5 O'clock P.M. I was quite unwell this evening with quinsy sore throat. I stopped at the Wilder Hotel for the night.

1. A former community in north central Linn County, Kan., Sec. 21 T19 R23, 8 miles northwest of LaCygne, occupied from 1859 to 1883.

2. Moneka, a former community 3 miles due north of Mound City, Kan.

3. Seat of Linn County, Kan.

4. Fort Lincoln, a Union picket post in northern Bourbon

County, on the Little Osage River, just west of present Fulton, Kan.

Friday, January 27. I found some of my Company this morning who had come prepared to take me to Camp Insley 12 miles east of Fort Scott. I rode out to Camp this forenoon, and received a happy greeting from my Company. I bought a full demi-john from the Fort and soon I had a camp of jolly fellows. I found all well, but the camp and horses in bad condition. The old recruits were quite jubilant over the idea of being mustered out of service soon and sent to their homes, as their term of service had about expired. . . .

Saturday, January 28. I remained in camp this forenoon and had my quarters thoroughly renovated and cleaned preparatory to my occupying them. I found a great lack of cleanliness throughout the camp owing to dereliction of duty on the part of the officer in command during my absence. I ordered my men too [sic] at once put their quarters in order. I rode out three miles this afternoon to visit my sister-in-law Mrs. Angie McPherson and found them well. I remained with them until near night, when I returned to camp. I have spent the evening with my Company. I find my room as more the appearance of health and comfort than last evening. Day pleasant.

Sunday, January 29. . . . I learn that no enemy has been seen of late in the near locality of our camp. The boys are spoiling for a little excitement of some kind. I think a good lively skirmish with the bush whacking gentry would be a desirable thing for us at this time, as I have been deprived of a luxury of the kind for a long period myself, and there is no prospect of finding any other game of larger dimensions from the enemy in Missouri very soon. Day very pleasant.

Monday, January 30. . . . Some of the boys have been busy getting up a dance at McPhersons tonight, three miles from town. I was tendered an invitation. At night I was accompanied by some of my company to the party. We found quite a number had arrived and many yet to come. I have not felt very well since my return, but will try the dance for a remedy and cure of my ills. The dance was soon set in motion by music furnished by Ogden Gray[1] and W. D. Porter of my Company. I was honored with Miss Alice Evans company in dancing the first set in a quadrille.

1. Corporal Ogden Gray, Baraboo, Wis., blacksmith.

Tuesday, January 31. The dance continued nearly all night. There was 24 couple that took part in the festivities of the occasion, and all was conducted in an orderly manner. I enjoyed myself very satisfactory, but did not feel well. After breakfast I returned to Camp. I took a good dose of whiskey and ginger on my arrival in camp as I am very unwell with a cold. I have not been busy at anything to day. I lay in bed this afternoon, and having no other remedy at hand, I took the whiskey and ginger after laying down. Day cloudy and rainy. *(Feb. 1 is omitted.)*

Thursday, February 2. This morning at 2 O'clock I rode to Fort Scott arrived at 5 O'clock this morning. I reported at the Hospital to Surgeon Van Duyne[1] who examined my case and informed me that my condition was such that I could not report at Paola [*as ordered*] and gave me the necessary medicine, and telegraphed Genl Blunt of my condition, and relieved me from going to Paola. I was obliged to keep in bed all day at the Wilder House. . . . *(Feb. 3 is omitted.)*

1. Believed to be Alfred Van Durn (spelling uncertain), assistant surgeon of the post.

Saturday, February 4. . . . I took my departure at once in company with 2nd Lieut. Eli M. Cooper and others of my Company who had remained in the Fort all night. On my way to Camp I took dinner at Mrs. Orrs a kind and good lady. After dinner we started to camp, but was obliged to swim our horses over the Marmaton river, as it was rising very fast from recent rains. I managed so I did not get very wet as my horse Dick is a good swimmer. I found all unusually quiet in camp after Pay-day. . . . *(Feb. 5-12 are omitted.)*

Monday, February 13. I rode out to John McPhersons this afternoon, as I learn that he is sick. John is a member of my Company. I found him quite sick. I returned to camp at dark and found the big Drywood and Marmaton rivers a rising, as there has been a heavy rain all day. I have spent the evening reading. The boys are in their quarters playing cards and indulging in other amusements, and getting away with Uncle Sams rations.

Tuesday, February 14. Rain heavy all night. I sent Alonzo Wheeler[1] of my Company to Fort Scott to procure medicine for John McPherson. He returned at noon, could not get the medicine to John, as too high water by the Drywood to cross with safety. So I was oblige to postpone until tomorrow what should be done to day. I have occupied my time writing to day. Stormy all day. *(Feb. 15-19 are omitted.)*

1. Private Alonzo Wheeler, Ironton, Wis.

Monday, February 20. It has been rainy all day, which has again raised the streams out of their banks. Communication to all points is now cut off for the present, and the demons of the brush are safe from molestation. I have no news to relate.

Tuesday, February 21. . . . I was most happy to receive a Telegram from Bettie to day stating that she was at Wyandotte, Kas. and could not come to me as there was no stages running on account of impassable roads. . . . *(Feb. 22-23 are omitted.)*

Friday, February 24. . . . Mr. True leader of Post Band was killed to night, by parties unknown.[1] *(Feb. 25-27 are omitted.)*

1. Fort Scott newspapers unlocated for this date.

Tuesday, February 28. . . . [*At Balltown*] I then walked up to Mr. Austins and visited the young ladies, Misses Mary, Martha and Ellen Dodge, and Miss Emaline Garrison. . . . The family very cordially invited me to return and stay during the night, which I finally accepted. . . . After Mr. Austin conducted family prayer I retired for the night. Day pleasant but very cool.

Wednesday, March 1. I spent the forenoon at Wm. Austins,[1] after a prolonged visit at this place, fraught with many attractions, I took my departure to my company. It rained some before I arrived in camp. Today cloudy windy and muddy.

1. Presumably Josiah M. Austin's, as usual; probably a transcriber's error.

Thursday, March 2. Many of the boys in the company had procured a supply of Family Disturber, which created an unusual commotion in camp. In fact it required a great amount of work on my part to enforce discipline and subordination. Michael Kivel and Martin Fillhouse[1] of my Company became involved in a quarrel in consequence of too much of the disturbing element in camp, and during the afternoon they engaged in a knock-down argument, but no blood stained field marked the spot where the combats were engaged. I have been making out Company Monthly Returns to day. . . . *(Mar. 3-9 are omitted.)*

1. Private Martin Fillhouer, Baraboo, Wis.

Friday, March 10. . . . I am anxious to have a call at any time from the bushwhacking rabble, so that a little excitement can be experienced for a change. The wind is fast drying the mud and the weather quite pleasant. *(Mar. 11-14 are omitted.)*

Wednesday, March 15. I have spent the day in Fort Scott. After transacting my business, I joined some army officers and had a jolly good time the remainder of the day. My wife arrived on stage from Wyandotte Kas. I was happy too meet her and little Mollie again. We stay at the Wilder House to night. Today some rainy.

Thursday, March 16. This morning I took wife and Mollie in ambulance to Fort Insley, my camp. We stopped at Betties fathers and took dinner, and then went to camp this afternoon, where Bettie receives her first initiation in the life of a soldier. The boys are pleased with the new recruit. Today cold with sleet and snow. *(Mar. 17-19 are omitted.)*

Monday, March 20. Today very cloudy and more indications of rain. This afternoon many of the boys was out of camp to bring their lady partners in to the dance. At dark the boys had brought all the fair sex of the neighborhood in, and the dance was soon began at once, also the rain began to add more moisture to the earth. As this was an occasion for enjoyment, my wife and self joined in the festivities of the occasion. *(Mar. 21-25 are omitted.)*

Sunday, March 26. The weather continues unfavorable and the day very cloudy and rainy. I find nothing to excite a person in mind or body at our post, but we are trying to be encourage[d] with the thought that this kind of weather can not be long duration, and the season of a soldiers bliss will return, with the dense thicket serving as the lair for the bush-whacking gentry to occupy our attention and the escorting of Major Genls and Pay Masters to Forts Gibson and Smith. *(Mar. 27-Apr. 1 are omitted.)*

Sunday, April 2. Today Bud Evans (my wifes brother) came to visit us. He is a fine young man of whom I think a parent should be proud of. We are enjoying fine weather now, only we would willingly part with our mud. I have no news to give to day.

Monday, April 3. This morning I sent a detail of eleven men as per request of Capt. Carpenter to join him with a portion of his Company and a detail from Co. "D" of our Regt who are to go in pursuit of some bushwhackers that the Captain says have raised hell promiscuously near Nevada. I had some difficulty getting my horses over the river on account of high water, but succeeded in getting my men and horses over all safe. Today some cloudy and chilly, but tolerable pleasant. *(Apr. 4 is omitted.)*

Wednesday, April 5. My men returned from the scout this afternoon and report an exciting adventure. They struck the trail of the enemy at

Nevada which took a south course. After following it all day yesterday until late in the evening, they found their game in an old house in the edge of some timber. The evening was very dark so the Captain charged the place from all sides. On reaching the house, the Enemy, nine in number opened fire through doors and windows at our men, killing one of my mens horses, but none were injured of our men. The men returned the fire killing one of the enemy and wounding a child slightly as a family was in the house.[1] Those of the enemy not killed made their escape in the darkness. The Scouts captured eleven horses and equipments and camped in the house during the night. . . . *(Apr. 6-9 are omitted.)*

1. One can imagine how much less lightly the diarist—having righteously reminded us that the "bushwhacking rabble" make war on women and children, egad!—would have treated the incident had roles been reversed.

Monday, April 10. I went to Fort Scott this morning to turn over some worn out and disabled horses, and draw fresh ones. On attempting to ride one of the new horses he reared and plunged finally falling. I was caught and under him and seriously hurt in the breast by my foot hanging in the stirrup and horse falling on me, there was firing of cannon in honor of the surrender of Genl Robert E. Lee and the Army of Northern Virginia to Lieut. Genl U.S. Grant. 200 guns were fired at Fort Scott. . . .

Tuesday, April 11. I have been confined to my

bed to day from great pain in my chest by horse falling on me yesterday. I have been unable to attend to business to day. I have applied for remedies procured at Hospital but get no relief so far. No more news of importance to day. The back bone of the Confederacy is broken, and we feel too rejoice, as the prospects are we are soon to lay down our arms and return to our peaceful avocations. To day some cloudy, but no rain.

Wednesday, April 12. . . . Many citizens have came in camp to learn if the reports are true as to Genl Lees surrender. . . . *(Apr. 13-14 are omitted.)*

Saturday, April 15. I received a dispatch this forenoon from Head Quarters, Fort Scott, that President Abraham Lincoln died this morning at 7 O'clock from pistol shot by the hand of John Wilkes Booth last evening at a few minutes past 10 o'clock in Fords Theater at Washington, D.C. While we was rejoicing over the downfall of the Confederacy, we are suddenly called upon to mourn the untimely end of our revered President. This has been a pleasant day otherwise.

Sunday, April 16. This morning I rode in company of Ex-Lieut Willsey and B. H. Johnson[1] of my Company to Fort Scott. On our arrival we found a large assemblage of people on the square attentively listening to an oration on the death of our President. Cannon was fired every half hour from the sun rising to its setting, and all government Buildings in the Fort were heavily draped in mourning, also all business and private buildings presented emblems of mourning, and flags were at half mast. . . . *(Apr. 17-21 are omitted.)*

1. Private Bennett H. Johnson, Madison, Wis.

Saturday, April 22. . . . We hear no more of the bushwhacking fraternity. Their delectable avocation they find not suitable in our territory. . . .

Sunday, April 23. My Company are getting restive for want of more employment, and I begin to think our last shot has been fired at the "Johnnies." What will be our destiny I can not tell. I have been idle to day. . . . *(Apr. 24-26 are omitted.)*

Thursday, April 27. I went to Fort Scott to day on business connected with my Company. Henry R. Turney[1] Hospital Steward at the Fort, and a member of my company accompanied me. On arriving at the Fort, I went to Hospital and Henry put me up some medicine for my infirmities. I then attended to my business and returned to camp this evening. I did not learn anything new while in the Fort. To day some cloudy.

1. Private Henry B. Turney, Baraboo, Wis., made Hospital Steward Mar.1.

Friday, April 28. . . . I have worked through many difficulties this day, as the mosquitoes have kept up a lively raid upon my face and hands. These pests are of large proportions, and their bite causes an intolerable burning and itching of the flesh beyond a Christian endurance and I have indulged in no small amount of vile language to give force too the supreme disgust I have for these Hell begotten tormenters. With the exception of mosquitoes the day has been pleasant. *(Apr. 29-May I are omitted.)*

Tuesday, May 2. . . . I find that the Mosquitoes have been reinforced by a large reserve of flies, whose biting qualities are of a superior kind, and a terror to man and beast. I am of the opinion that no Christianity exist in this camp since our late tormenters have arrived. Day some cloudy. *(May 3-7 are omitted.)*

Monday, May 8. . . . My Company dancers, have arranged for a dance in camp to night and have been out among the citizens to procure the ladies for the occasion. The dance commenced at an early hour. Among the fair sex who grace the occasion are Mrs. Sample, Snelson and Miss Mollie Daughtety, Miss Alice Evans and Angie Snelson. Fine weather now.

Tuesday, May 9. The dance continued until day light this morning. Good order prevailed through the night. This morning I broke up my residence in Fort Insley, and packed up my baggage to take my departure for Fort Leavenworth to muster as Captain of Co "F" 3rd Wis. Cav. and procure my pay from Government. My wifes father and wife came to bid us farewell as we do not expect to return to this camp again. My wife and her child and Miss Alice Evans accompany me to Fort Scott this morning and L. P. Luce also. We stop at the Wilder House to day. To day very rainy. *(May 10 is omitted.)*

Thursday, May 11. This morning at 7 o'clock I took passage on Stage for Kansas City and Leavenworth. My wife and daughter, Lieut Luce and Miss Alice Evens was in Company. We arrived at Paola, Kans. At 5½ o'clock P.M. Day pleasant.

Friday, May 12. This morning at 7 o'clock we again resume our journey arrived at Olathe, Kansas, where we took dinner. After dinner my wife and daughter, and Miss Alice took Stage for Kans. City and Independence Mo. Lieut. [Leonard] Luce and myself took Stage for Leavenworth City at the St. George Hotel at 5½ o'clock P.M. Day pleasant.

Saturday, May 13. Lieut. Luce and myself procured conveyance to Fort Leavenworth where I was mustered in Captain and Luce 1st Lieut. Co. "F" 3d Wis. Cav. My muster dates from March 9th 1865. We was mustered by Major Wm. O. Gould, 14th Kan. Vol. Cav. and Asst Commissary of Musters. We returned to the City this afternoon when I witnessed a shooting affray on the street between Col. Jennison and Major Anthony at 4 o'clock P.M. Jennison received a wound in the thigh. Anthony escaped unhurt.[1] Pleasant day. *(May 14-24 are omitted.)*

1. A classic case of thieves falling out. Certainly fellow-Jayhawkers Charles R. Jennison and Daniel R. Anthony (Susan B. Anthony's brother) deserved each other. Alas, Jennison (along with an innocent bystander) was only slightly wounded, and in Radical Kansas neither man suffered unduly from the law or public opinion.—Stephen Z. Starr, *Jennison's Jayhawkers,* Baton Rouge, Louisiana State U. Press, 1973, 380-81.

Friday, May 25. I went out in the City a short time this forenoon but not feeling well I returned to my boarding place, feeling that my country did not require my services any longer, and disease was manifesting an unyielding supremacy over my once robust constitution. I was hesitating in my mind as too [sic] my duty. This afternoon I wrote out and sent in my Resignation as Captain of Co. "F" 3d Wis. Vol. Cav. I attended Theater again to night. The play was excellent. Day very hot. *(May 26-31 are omitted.)*

Thursday, June 1. . . . Col. David S. Vittum arrived at the St. George Hotel this evening from Fort Scott. He informed me that my Company and others of the Battalion are enroute to Fort Leavenworth and are expected to arrive tomorrow. The Colonel says he thinks the entire Companies will be sent out on the plains. Today very hot. *(June 2 is omitted.)*

Saturday, June 3. I went up to the Fort this morning and found my Company all well. The boys did not like the idea of their being sent out west, as they claim that it was not in the contract to fight Indians, and the close of the war terminated their service. But go they must. After spending the day with my Company, I returned to the City. To day very windy and dusty. *(June 4-5 are omitted.)*

Tuesday, June 6. . . . Reports which are authentic, are that Company "C" are in a mutinous condition and have damaged their Capt. James B. Ponds personal property, by shearing his horses mane and tail, destroying his fine Saddle and bridle, Broke his Sabre, and stole his two fine ivory stocked Revolvers, and notifying him that his life would be taken if he remained in Company. . . .

Porter spent the following month in idleness at Leavenworth, occasionally assigned some administrative duty, and waiting impatiently for his resignation to be accepted.

Thursday, July 6. . . . I was made happy this afternoon by the arrival of my wife and little Mollie from Independence, Mo. This evening I received the Acceptance of my Resignation as Capt. Co. "F" 3d Wis. Cav. dated June 19th 1865. I am this evening no longer in the Military service of the United States, and am once more free from Military rule and despotism. Another hot day. *(July 7-10 are omitted.)*

Tuesday, July 11. At 11 o'clock this morning I took my departure with all I possessed, from the City of Leavenworth on the Steam boat Emily for Kansas City, Mo. I arrived there at 3 o'clock P.M. There being no conveyance going to Independence to day, so my wife and self decided to go up to Wyandotte and spend the night with Mr. Hallford and family who keep the Garno House. We rode over in a Burs [?], and found our friends extending their former kind hospitality. . . .

Wednesday, July 12. This morning we took a final leave of our friends and returned to Kansas City where we remained until 3 o'clock P.M. We then took conveyance on the cars to Independence, where we arrived at 3½ o'clock P.M. at the residence of John E. Scruggs,[1] my brother in law. We found all well, and extending a happy greeting. . . . *(July 13-16 are omitted.)*

1. John E. Scruggs, born Tennessee 1833; in 1855 he entered the mercantile business at Papinsville in Bates County, but returned to Jackson County in 1861 and farmed; at the war's end he moved into Independence. In 1843 "a man named Scruggs" (relationship, if any, unknown) had settled in Badger Township but after only a few years moved to Van Buren, Ark.—*History of Vernon County,* 432.

Monday, July 17. I accompanied my wife and her sister Alice down in town and visited a Picture gallery where we had some pictures taken. After leaving the gallery we visited some other places of interest, and returned to Mr. Scruggs, Wife and Alice was pleased with the places visited, though I took no interest in what I have seen to day. . . . *(July 18 is omitted.)*

Wednesday, July 19. This morning I procured a conveyance to take our departure from Independence, Mo. With my little family we bade Mr. Scruggs and family and Miss Alice Evans farewell, and started on our homeward journey for Wisconsin. We arrived at Wayne City landing[1] on the Missouri river, three miles distant from Independence in due time. There being no Steam boat at the landing, enroute to St. Louis, we found good accommodations at a private family near bye, where we will wait for the arrival of a boat. . . .

1. Wayne City or Upper Independence Landing, founded before the 1850s, was later connected to Independence by macadamized road.

Thursday, July 20. At an early hour this morning we were aroused from our slumbers by a Steam boat whistle. We made hurried preparation, and took passage on the Steamer "Marcella" at 4½ o'clock this morning, Greenleaf was the Captain.

Friday, July 21. . . . Arrived at the landing at St. Louis at 9½ o'clock P.M.

Saturday, July 22. . . . At 6 o'clock this morning we took the cars for Chicago . . . arrived at Chicago at 8 o'clock this evening. We put up at the Eagles Hotel at N.W. Depot. . . . *(July 23 is omitted.)*

Monday, July 24. At 9 o'clock this morning we took passage on the cars for Madison, Wis. after a pleasant days journey we arrive at Madison at 3 o'clock P.M. I saw a number of soldiers of Baraboo, my home place who have just returned from the army to [be] mustered out. I stop at the American House to night. Beverly Jefferson is Proprietor, and my army companion on Co. "S" 1st Wis. In.

Tuesday, July 25. This morning at 7 o'clock we took conveyance on James Cowles Stage for Baraboo 40 miles distant. Arrived at Lodi at 2 o'clock P.M. and took dinner. Soon after dinner, we was again jogging on our way. At about sunset we arrived at home, where Mother after a long waiting received her last son from the army. Thus I have recorded an account of my service to my country, and some incidents coming under my observation in brief besides a short account of some of the most important skirmishes and battles I participated in, besides fatiguing marches through heat & cold, and the innumerable privations of army life, and my final return to my home. I shall make some farther additions to complete this Record.[1]. . .

1. The "farther additions" consisted of copies of some of Porter's personal orders, plus roster and organizational chart for Company F, which was finally mustered out of service at Madison, Wis., October 12, 1865.

❦ APPENDIX ❦

3rd Wisconsin Troopers Who Married Locally During or After Their Vernon County Service

Lieutenant Charles W. Porter, Co F - Mrs. Bettie Evans Rowntree, Dec. 4, 1864.

Private Alexander Preston, Co F - Widow Woodruff, Aug. 13, 1864.

Major Benjamin S. Henning, 2nd Bn - "Fort Scott lady," May 5, 1864.

Corporal Origin Royce Benedict, Co A - Martha Lydia Dodge, Dec. 6, 1864.

Corporal Marion Mason Clough, Co A - Harriet Ellen Dodge, Dec. 2, 1865.

Captain Robert R. Carpenter, Co A - Mary Elizabeth Dodge, Apr. 23, 1868.

Private John Richardson, Co A - Malinda Charles, Jan. 21, 1864.

Corporal Lewis P. Harris, Co A - Mary Jane Wilson, Jan. 21, 1864.

Corporal Simeon Bennett Davis, Co F - Sarah Emaline Garrison, June 17, 1866.

Private John McPherson, Co F - Angie Evans, Apr. 24, 1864.

Corporal Joseph H. Waddell, Co F (unconfirmed but was a postwar resident of Deerfield and had a child there).

INDEX